Dear Theresa

We will always be

A BONDED FRIENDSHIP

Moses and Eliphalet

Bonded in Friendship

Gretchel Hathaway

by

Gretchel Hathaway, PhD

Lexingford Publishing LLC
New York Ottawa San Francisco Hong Kong
www.lexingfordpublishingllc.com

ISBN-13: 978-09981665-0-6
ISBN-10: 0998166502

Registered and deposited in the Library of Congress

Photographic credits: Cover photograph and Author photograph by Matt Milless

Set in Cambria 12

Printed and Published in the United States of America

First Edition

Lexingford Publishing LLC
New York Ottawa San Francisco Hong Kong
www.lexingfordpublishingllc.com

Celebrating *A Bonded Friendship*: *Moses and Eliphalet*

We all know about Frederick Douglass and his path to freedom. This book provides a wonderful opportunity to learn about another man from the same Maryland county who crossed the Choptank River to escape slavery and find a better future. The remarkable story of Moses Viney and his relationship with one of the nation's leading college presidents both inspires us and provides new insight into a challenging period in our nation's history.

Freeman A. Hrabowski, III
President, the University of Maryland, Baltimore County

Probably because they lived far from the African coast, my Nigerian ancestors were not pressed into slavery. *A Bonded Friendship* has been enjoyable and valuable to me in seeing, through Moses Viney's eyes, the desperate dilemma of American slaves as well as their courage in seeking freedom. This is a memorable and important book, especially for its multi-faceted view of the long and heartfelt friendship between Moses Viney and Union College President Eliphalet Nott.

Kehinde Dunsin, PhD
Author, *Shibli*

The story of Moses Viney - his birth on a Maryland plantation, a dangerous escape from slavery via the Underground Railroad, employment at Schenectady's Union College, and achievements as an entrepreneur - stands as a testament to his courage, intelligence and humanity. Gretchel Hathaway's book affords us a unique opportunity to become acquainted with Mr. Viney as an important historical figure who succeeded in facing overwhelming odds in his odyssey from slavery to freedom. It will prove to be an essential book for readers of all ages and will make an excellent addition to any library that values American and African-American history.

Neil B. Yetwin (retired), Historian
Department of Social Studies
Schenectady High School

Dedication

This book is dedicated to my children, Rachel Linnice Avelina Tyson and Stephen Joseph Tyson, Jr., my parents and my grandmother, Louise Hathaway. May the spirits of our ancestors keep us safe, grounded, humble and eager to learn as we continue to make the world a better place.

Acknowledgments

The list of folks I need to acknowledge and thank could be endless. The people below have played an integral part of this writing journey. I appreciate their time, encouragement, constructive criticism and words of wisdom that kept me moving forward with the manuscript. I'm sure there are others, please forgive the mind but you are in my heart. A special thank you to:

Kathy Mackel, Director of Caroline Office of Tourism, Maryland; Neil Yetwin, Historian; Bernard McEvoy, MD and the Volunteers of Vale Cemetery, Schenectady NY; Hamilton Hill Arts Center, Schenectady NY; Schenectady Historical Society staff and volunteers; Walter Simpkins – actor and community leader; Susan Perkins, Editor; Shawn Whitehead, minister and historian; Dayle Smith who introduced me to my publisher; Kathy Delorenzo, editor; Brigham Taylor, editor; Stephen Schmidt, economist; Strom Thacker and Jermaine Wells – hand models; and Union College Special Collections staff and photographer. In addition a very warm thank you to my dedicated supporters who gently encouraged the writing of this story throughout this process: Stephen C. Ainlay; Judith Gardner Ainlay; Victoria (Viki) Brooks; Jason Benitez; Caleb Northrop; Cyril Tyson; Sunchita Tyson; Rita Oliverio; Barbara Danowski; Robert and Barbara Holland; Angela Tatem; Deidre Hill Butler; Matt Milless, Cover Photographer; my siblings – Gary, Gregory, Geoffrey, Gloria; my children Rachel L. Tyson, Stephen J. Tyson, Jr. and my Grandmother Louise Hathaway. Although they were not here for the conception and birth of this book, I acknowledge my parents, Gloria and Garfield Hathaway and my ancestors some of whom were enslaved, walked the Trail of Tears, and who knows, may have crossed paths with Moses Viney on their journeys.

Preface

This book is historical fiction based on the true story of Eliphalet Nott, President of Union College and Moses Viney, an escaped slave who became Nott's driver and confidante during the 1800's. This is an accurate story of the relationship between Viney and Nott, with fictional elements added in since we have facts from Eliphalet's history, but very little is written about the life of Moses and his wife, Anna.

The story of Moses Viney and Eliphalet Nott was brought to my attention by a local high school history professor, Neil Yetwin. As a teacher, Neil wanted to get his very diverse students, local youngsters from Schenectady High School in NY, interested in history and excited about their community. He not only shared this story, but also the story of finding Moses' gravesite in what was originally called the "Colored Plot" in the Vale Cemetery. Neil brought his students to the site and cleaned up the debris and rubbish from the area.

Planting trees and removing weeds brought notice to the site, which is now called the Ancestral Plot. In addition, Union College students and local churches raised funds to place a tombstone on the gravesites of Moses and Anna Viney. The Moses Viney story is reenacted every year during Juneteenth, the celebration on June 16, 1865 that commemorates the end of slavery. Juneteenth is hosted by Dr. Bernard MacEvoy and Mr. Walter Simpkins of the Vale Cemetery and the Hamilton Hill Arts Center in Schenectady, NY, respectively. The use of oral history with historical facts allows our community to remember and appreciate the unique relationship between Viney and Nott.

I am very careful about language. There are words used in history that I decided I could not use in a book, but I also could not alter history. I chose not to use modern words like black or African American. These are words that would not have been stated during the slave era. Therefore, I use the word colored or negro to identify African American descent. Language is important; I chose not to use derogatory language such as the "N'" word. Though used during the slavery period, it is a difficult word for me to even write the letter representing the word, let alone share. One day, I pray that in our world and in all languages, all derogatory words for race, gender identity and expression, culture, ability and religion are erased from all vocabulary.

I welcome contact with my readers through my publisher, www.lexingfordpublishingllc.com.

November 1, 2016
Gretchel L. Hathaway, Ph.D.
Dean of Diversity and Inclusion
Chief Diversity Officer
Union College
Schenectady, NY 12308

Table of Contents

Table of Contents, cont.

Table of Contents, cont.

Chapter One

A Relationship of Trust

Have you ever taken the time to look at your friendships and relationships with others and wonder how and why you are so close? Relations are good to have with people you can depend on, or who are dependent on you. Relations are difficult; you have to work on them to keep them good and healthy. I've had many relations that started out good and sweet but went sour over time. I've had many relations that I was fearful to start but grew comfortable when I got to know the person.

This is my story. I'm an escaped slave working for one of the most important and intelligent men in the free land, Eliphalet Nott, president of Union College in Schenectady, NY. How we wound up together is a story of a relationship of trust. Upon hearing some of his speeches to students and his preaching I know that he is against slavery and the laws that keep it in the Southern states.

While I was a slave, I had good relations with some and poor relations with others. As a young'un, I had a good relationship with the son of my master. We started out as babes playing and learning together, but our relationship changed over time, which is expected once you get to school age. But he, the young Master Murphy, changed for the worse, especially after his pa died. He became hard and mean. And 'cause of his behavior, I became worried about my life, my future, my freedom. And in my mind as I got older, I would have the song in my head that I heard my family sing in the back fields beyond the ear of the white man:

> No more auction block for me, no more no more
> No more auction block for me, many a thousand gone
>
> No more peck of corn for me, no more no more
> No more peck of corn for me, many a thousand gone
>
> No more hundred lash for me, no more no more
> No more hundred lash for me, many a thousand gone

Though I am an escaped slave, my freedom is always at jeopardy, even in this free state. I don't worry every day about being brought back into slavery, but there are stories of escaped slaves and truly free negro men being kidnapped and brought back to the deep South. This is what I fear the most, never to be seen again, and no one knowing whether I am alive or dead. And now this fear is real and has grasped my heart into my bones as I take my horse and buggy into town on a small errand for President Nott.

The Moment of Discovery

As I saw him from my carriage, I looked back twice blinking my eyes. It couldn't have been him. I moved towards the back of my carriage where he couldn't see me. He's talking to a couple in front of the Givens Hotel in Schenectady. He's rounder than the last time I saw him and he's wearing a beard, but it looks like him. The streets are busy with people bustling around and no one realizes the importance of this man who looks like a local farmer. I can't believe he is here; I must leave and my safe haven is a few miles away. I can barely hear what he is saying to the townspeople, my neighbors. He is showing them a paper, but the people are walking away from him. I hear him as he gets more angry:

"Do you know this Negroid man named Moses Viney? He stands straight and strong, $50 reward for this negro, who stands above five feet tall. He has a bushy head, keeps it very nicely combed. He has been raised in the house so he speaks good. I expect he works for a family as a butler or house servant. He is my slave in Maryland. He escaped and I've heard he's here in Schenec'dy."

Well, that's when I realized that he is here to get me. He is here for me... to reclaim me, to enslave me, to take away my freedom. I hear him – it's the junior Master Murphy, my former "slave owner." I hear him say and he repeats my name:

"Moses is an escaped slave and I am here to retrieve my property – this is the law."

I see people avoiding him, while some have stopped to ask him questions. I wait, breaking out into a cold sweat, wanting to run, flee, to get away, but I'm frozen in my tracks knowing that if I make a move the junior Richard Murphy, my former master's son, will see me and, if he retrieves me, I will either die or my world will be in chains.

THE GARNET, 1910 281

Schenectady, Dec. 5th 1850.

This certifies that Moses Viney, a colored man, has been in my employment for eight years. He leaves the United States on account of the late fugitive slave law. He is a man of great integrity, and great industry and capability. He is a moral and religious man in whom entire confidence can be placed. Should the funds he has taken not be sufficient for his support till he gets employment, he is hereby authorized to draw on me at sight at the Mohawk Bank at Schenectady, State of New York, for any sum not exceeding one hundred dollars, and I will honor the draft.

Eliphalet Nott Pres.

"Schenectady December 5th, 1850
This certifies that Moses Viney, a colored man has been in my employment for eight years. He leaves the United States on account of the late fugitive slave law. He is a man of great integrity, and great industry and capability. He is a moral and religious man in whom entire confidence can be found. Should the funds he has taken not be sufficient for his support till he gets employment, he is hereby authorized to draw on me at sight at the Mohawk Bank of Schenectady, State of New York, for any sum not exceeding one hundred dollars and I will honor the draft. Eliphalet Nott, Pres." Reprinted in *The Garnet,* 1910, a Union College publication.

Chapter Two

A Life in 'Chains'

I don't really remember being in chains. I am suddenly aware that feelings of anxiety that I had when I was younger were feelings put on me by my shackles – my mind was in chains, my intelligence was stifled, my movements were controlled. Yes, I saw family relations and other slaves in iron chains – their ankles cut deep from the weight of the metal with only inches to move around as they slept on the floor. On the Murphy plantation, slaves were only chained when they were first brought to the farm or if they disobeyed the master.

My master, the senior Mr. Murphy, was a good master. Rarely did he order a beating for a slave and he kept the slave families together. I knew this was rare. My pa said he knew of youngsters being taken away from their mothers when they were old enough to be farmhands and fathers sold to other farms away from their wives. We were allowed to visit family on other farms, but these visits were controlled, quick trips and we had to earn trust to ensure that we would return. Pa said this trust is to remain solid, never to be broken or Master will withhold this privilege and others on the farm will suffer. Our chains were invisible, but I realized that my ankles were cuffed and locked as I watched the Murphys' with their freedom to come and go, and I ached to be able to walk away from the plantation without fear. I didn't know where I would go, but I wanted freedom to come. I knew there was so much to learn, so much in the world, but my mind was shackled and limited to the work I was forced to do to survive. There was so much out in the world; I heard the Murphys talk about trains, cities, and the northern Yankees. They complained about Northerners wanting slaves free. They protested:

"How do those dang Northerners know what my slaves want? The slaves don't know what they want. Our slaves are happy here."

I watched young Master Murphy as he continued down the street, with his determined walk from the Givens hotel, making his proclamation about the return of his slave, his property. I wondered if he realizes that the people he is talking to do not want slavery as he continues asking them questions. His back is turned to me, so I jump into my carriage, and slowly but swiftly head back to my safe haven at the college. I decide I need to talk to the only person I trust in this town, the man whose speeches I've listened to many times. He had once owned slaves, this I knew, but now he has spoken against slavery. He feels remorse about his family once owning slaves and his speeches tell the story of the immoral reasons against it.

Trusting Minister Eliphalet Nott

I am the messenger and driver of the president of the college. We have a mutually respectful relationship. In one of his speeches, he speaks to young men about the abolition of slavery. He talks about making moral decisions; and though he's never stated that he is an abolitionist, he speaks against slavery. His name is Eliphalet Nott, a minister and president of Union

College. He is a kind man who speaks against slavery. He is very passionate about speaking on the many problems with prohibition and his lectures help students better understand the consequences of decisions because he is able to look at an argument from many sides. He seems to have special relations with all of his present and past students. Some students are against slavery and are members of the Union College abolitionist student group called The Antislavery Society, which started in 1836. Other students from the South want slavery. I must explain my circumstances to Dr. Nott. I never told him that I escaped and I don't know why I didn't tell him. He is the only person I can trust and who has the means to help me.

Chapter Three

So Much at Stake

As I do my work around the college, I begin to take in all that I could lose if I return to slavery in Maryland. The president lives with students in a building on campus called South College and I have a nice room all to myself in the same building. South College sits at the edge of campus, to be close to the city as well as part of the college. Schenectady lies between three waterways, Schoharie Creek, Normans Kill and the Mohawk River, which bleeds into the Hudson River and has lots of good fishin'. The hills of Schenectady are called Yautapuch-aberg, taken from the French and Indians. These hills had a few wheat farms for pasturage, but most folks worked in the city. I learned all this from my talks with Dr. Nott. He teaches me a lot and I have good memories. I also learn some of these things from the students. I try to learn new things and new words every day.

Dr. Nott is still designing this campus. He planned for the campus to be thought out carefully. South College is where we live with these smart but growing boys. Dr. Nott and his Missus live in six rooms, which make up his housing. Many of the faculty and their families live in buildings with students as well. We are comfortable being around the boys.

Dr. Nott and I work well together. There are times when he shares with me the many issues he's handling, not just about the college, but also about the nation in which we live. Dr. Nott is an inventor, as matter of fact, he invented the stove that warms us in our home. He is close to many politicians, powerful people in their states.

Well, I knew I must talk with Dr. Nott today. I wait to approach him until the sunset when his college work is finished 'cause of his busy dealings for the college. I watch for the light to go out in his library as I peek from the hall. He is moving much slower lately, but he is full of life and his mind is sharp. Dr. Nott is a very intelligent man of integrity. He has a lot of worries lately, worries about a country dividing, worries about a possible war and that our students may have to give up their education to fight for our country. He also has a lot of campus work to do. He was the president of two colleges—Union College and the trade school Rensselaer Institute since1829. For years he worked for both institutions, but recently gave up his service at Rensselaer, which was now strong enough to become a college in its own right. I think doing both jobs may have taken a toll on his health and his rheumatism, a disease that hurts his muscles and aches through to his bones.

He also wants our students to be well-rounded citizens—a term used to make certain the students studied hard. It does not mean "big and fat" like I thought. And on many occasions I have to request the presence of a misdirected student to meet with him. When a student is not doing well in courses or is caught misbehaving, I am told to retrieve the student from his quarters to bring him to Dr. Nott. Usually the student is nervous, shaking a little and rubbing his hands. I see his discomfort and first I say to him is "What you did is not right."

Most times I don't know what he did, but this usually gets him talking fast. After he confesses, I make suggestions:

"Be honest with Dr. Nott. Look him straight in the eye, remove your cap, and make sure you tell him your problems in a calm, humble manner. Remember you were the one in the wrong, so show remorse for your behavior. Look at your shoes and say you're sorry. Show him respect and say 'yes sir' and 'no sir.' "

Nott is usually stern initially upon greeting a student and more of a teacher when the conversation is over. He is well respected by both students and faculty. Nott handles many legal issues on campus and raises funds for the school, which rumor has it, is not doing well financially. He also offers very good lectures and speeches on the campus on national issues, including politics, prohibition, slavery and other moral topics that he wants the students to know about.

Well, I decide to wait for Dr. Nott to sit in the room they call a parlor. He comes here for evening tea before heading to the comfort of bed. He lives with the students just like other professors on campus. There was room for him and Mrs. Nott to live in this building. He keeps watch over them, like a shepherd to his flock. I approach cautiously: "Good evening sir, it's time for your cup of tea before parting to rest?"

He looks up at me with caring eyes. "Moses, you know I have tea every evening before heading to sleep. You've been following me with your eyes all day. Is there something you wish to talk with me about?"

I am caught off guard by his directness and observations. He is always very aware of the people around him.

I begin to tell him about my life before I met him in Glenville, on Dr. Fonda's farm. Finally, I began sharing with him that I was an escaped slave and today when I was in town I saw my dead master's son, who became my master upon his death. I told Dr. Nott that I know that the young master is here because of the new slave law that all the folks and some students are talking about. He has come to reclaim his property—and that would be me, sir. Dr. Nott states in anger:

"It's the Fugitive Slave Law, which came about in 1850, where all escaped slaves are seen as fugitives because they left their owners for freedom. And now your owner has come to reclaim his property? This is outrageous."

He stands up, pacing the room, very upset by this news. I said to Dr. Nott, "I have had my thirst quenched by freedom for a few years and now I begin to feel my throat parched and dry in fear. I don't know how he has found out my location. I may never know, but one thing I do know is that I do not want to go back—I will die first."

Dr. Nott was not looking at me; he was looking through me as if his mind was already in motion. He was calm, but his neck and cheeks were slowly getting a red blush. He sternly said, "Reclaim his property. Reclaim his property!" He became agitated, but took in a deep breath and said, "How dare this man call another human being property?"

He sat in silence for a moment breathing deeply as he sipped his tea. He took a deep breath and said, "We need to get a good night's sleep. We can wait until the morning to call upon two friends of mine who understand this law in order to see what we could do to keep your freedom."

Dr. Nott also knew people like Gerrit Smith, a smart man who lectures on antislavery at the Schenectady Church and who gives money to abolitionists who broke the Fugitive Slave Law to help keep escaped slaves free.

Dr. Nott took the last sips of his tea with one gulp. He motioned to me to sit and said, "The sooner we get to bed, the sooner morning will come and we can deal with this problem."

I assisted Dr. Nott with getting his night clothes on. Though he was able to walk on his own, making his steps was getting harder for him. He seemed strong right now, as if he was ready for a fight. He leaned on me and held hard against the wall. Our slow but determined walk made me admire him more, as he assured me that things would be all right. I, on the other hand, was more worried. I had never shared my story with a white man before and he was the first and only white man I ended up ever trusting—except for the younger Mr. Murphy when he and I were childhood lads.

Eliphalet Nott, President of Union College for 62 years.
Union College Library Special Collections.

Chapter Four

Young Richard and I

Young Richard and I were born on the same day, but one year apart. My ma was his mammy and we were raised together. We played all day into the night. My pa said if it weren't for my colored skin color, we were like brothers. We ate our noon supper together and played with frogs. I taught him how to skip stones at the river. He taught me some of the things he was learning from his mom like reading and writing.

Although I was older than he was, I was slightly smaller than him and I also knew he had more power over me. There were times when we were caught doing something we weren't supposed to, where he would blame me and I knew to keep my mouth shut. My pa or some other field hand would smack me. But Ma, well, she knew the truth but also said nothing. Sometimes she would give me extra food to say that she was sorry for me. I was smarter than young Richard on some things, but he had book learning. And when he came of age, he got to go away every day to school and I had to stay on the farm. He was so angry with me that I got to stay with my ma. He didn't want to go to school and fought his ma every day. Sometimes he would get so mad he would hit my ma, his mammy, 'cause he didn't want to go. He wanted for nothing, had clothes, books and toys. I had my work pants with a torn but clean shirt for cool days, but no books, no toys. I wasn't jealous of him, but somehow I felt he was of me. By the time I was seven, we were no longer brothers. He had changed; we had grown apart and I didn't know why then.

Back in Schenectady and an Attorney's Decision

The next day, I heard Dr. Nott up earlier than usual. As I drew water for his morning bath, he handed me a note to bring to Attorney James Brown and another for Judge Douglass Campbell. The note asked them to come to the house on campus later that afternoon. I helped Dr. Nott dress and manage the walk to his small library. He is able to move better when the warm morning sun hits his room just right on a cool fall day. He has a determination in his walk on this day, not like his evening slow movements. I left him with his morning breakfast and went out to hitch up the horse and carriage.

Then I drove the carriage quickly to their big homes with white pillars, fences and pretty gardens. Both gentlemen said they would be on the campus by teatime, though it was Judge Campbell who was agitated that he didn't know why he was summoned, and I wasn't 'bout to tell him. When I got back, Dr. Nott asked me to walk him to the college library. He began pulling out old newspapers and books and writin' things down. He said he needed quiet and had to read and write quickly before the judge and attorney arrived.

We were back in South College when they arrived. They had long discussions in Dr. Nott's parlor while I served them teacakes and sandwiches. I stayed in the room standing by the mantel and only spoke to explain my circumstances. I didn't go into detail; I just let them know that I was fleeing from Denton, Maryland. I told my story:

"My two friends and I followed the Choptank River and headed north. We first wound up in Pennsylvania and then traveled towards Troy, New York. My friends wound up coming with me as I kept moving further north trying to get to Canada. Though I was in free land, I wanted to make sure my freedom was not taken away. I found labor work on the Fonda farm on the outskirts of a city in Glendale. At that time, I had difficulty with the name of Schenectady. And that's where Dr. Nott found and hired me."

What I didn't tell them about was my first meeting with Dr. Nott. I stopped talking at that time 'cause I didn't think they needed to know about it. Dr. Nott and I seemed to be respectful of each other. He liked me for my hard work and I think for my intelligence; I liked him for his brilliant mind and dedication to justice. I decided to stay in this bustling city on a campus of learning with a man I believed I could trust with my life. I don't know how I sensed this. I just trusted Dr. Nott's caring eyes and his soft-spoken nature.

Schenectady was a big city, offering new and different types of jobs. It was not like the plantation where every day was the same, every job depended on the need of the masters with most slaves doing the same work over and over. In Schenectady, many people worked in the broom factory. The Erie Canal brought many barges up and down the Mohawk River and the jobs were plentiful—from working on the river banks to lifting and loading items on the barges to local businesses. The railroad brought many people into town from Saratoga and other cities. Even the college was growing. I found out that the college had moved to this location from down in the city because it was getting more students. The new college campus was in the middle of our city, offering many good opportunities, churches, shopping and travel for the students and faculty—and for me.

Over the next few days, Dr. Nott had long conversations with the attorneys. Although sometimes I was present, they talked about the slave law and it was difficult to understand at times. Therefore, the decisions were in their hands. Finally, after four days of meetings, Dr. Nott and the attorneys realized that the only way for me to never return to slavery was to buy my freedom. This needed to be done in a businesslike manner. I was not to attend the deliberations with the young Master Murphy.

Neither would Dr. Nott attend so that he would not be associated with the sale or bargaining. Buying my freedom could cause trouble. Northern students would question buying a slave and the Southern students could say that Dr. Nott was freeing slaves. Therefore, Dr. Nott had to be careful to keep the talks secret. He would have his grandson, Clarkson N. Potter, handle the details of the sale and costs by contacting the young Master Murphy, letting him know that Dr. Nott wanted to buy my freedom and find out what amount he wanted. Mr. Potter left to meet my master with eagerness, proud of being placed with this responsibility. It took a few days for Mr. Potter to return on this first trip to bargain. In the meantime, I worked hard but slept little. At night I would hear the night animals outside my house and some nights I watched the moon rise and then the sun rise with no sleep between.

A few weeks later, as I walked to the carriage house, I noticed Mr. Potter's carriage outside the stables. I hurried back to South College, entering from the back door, to hear Dr. Nott talking in loud tones:

"That's outrageous! He wants his property back and wants an unreasonable sum of money! What does he think, humans are made of gold? This is not a reasonable sum. This is not right. This man has no morals! You can't own a man and you can't ask for an outrageous sum for his freedom!"

As I walked in, Dr. Nott immediately caught his composure and calmed down. He said in a less angry voice: "The master, Mr. Murphy, has requested the outrageous sum of $1,900 for your freedom when the normal fee is at the highest $800 for an able-bodied slave. Though no longer young, you could still be a good field hand, but the master knows that you would never be allowed to butler, nor be trusted, even if you were sold to another."

I realized that my master needed the money more than he needed a slave and he would rather wait and see how much he could get from Dr. Nott—a Yankee, he would call him. For my master, and those like him back home, calling someone a Yankee was akin to placing a curse on someone. I feared this would not be a gentlemanly exchange.

I did not have the fear or worry that other escaped slaves may have had—being scared that a white man may buy their freedom but then in turn keep them enslaved for themselves. I trusted Dr. Nott; he was always a man of his word and we have had a mutual bond long before this situation.

After receiving the news that my master wanted such a huge amount, Dr. Nott was concerned that he might come back secretly after me. Young Master Murphy knew where I was located and it would be easy for him to find me and force me back into slavery. Master Murphy was a proud man, not a man to be tricked by a runaway slave who ruined his reputation. The loss of a slave to escape was both a money issue and a personal embarrassment.

One of the reasons for the excessive price was probably due to changes with the master's income. The Murphy family had a stable plantation until the death of senior Master Murphy. There were three types of plantations in Denton. Strong plantations created a lot of money for the family and the masters had a lot of power in city government matters. The weak plantations were always on the edge of ruin so masters would beat their slaves severely for minor issues trying to get them to work harder and to put fear in them to keep them from escaping. On these plantations, many of these slaves would try to escape. It was common for many of the masters and their sons to bed the female slaves by force, whether they were married or not.

The Murphy family was in the middle, very stable and we had a kind-hearted master who took care of his slaves. Upon his death, under the rule of junior Master Murphy, the plantation was slowly starting to lose money. Young Master Murphy began to consider selling slaves off, which many of the house slaves heard in the family talk.

In the College parlor, we sat together to hear the story of Mr. Potter's journey. Dr. Nott, Mr. Potter, and I waited for Attorney Brown and Judge Campbell to discuss the options. Both briskly walked in; I took their coats and hats and stood at my place by the door. When everyone was seated, Dr. Nott asked me to take a seat at the table.

Dr. Nott said solemnly, "This is about your life. You take your seat at the table and listen closely."

It wasn't typical for a colored man to sit at the table with whites. I greatly appreciated Dr. Nott for this show of respect. Mr. Potter shared my master's story with these two men who were listening closely. It seems that my master was more upset that I took two other slaves with me and that he couldn't find either. Mr. Campbell and Mr. Brown directly asked Dr. Nott several questions about me, but Dr. Nott turned to me and asked me to answer the two gentlemen.

Some of the questions were good questions and were expected: "How long have you been on the run?" "Did you use the Underground Railroad?" "Did any family member join you?" Other questions made my stomach feel queasy: "Did you take anything from the home that didn't belong to you?" "Did you hurt anyone before you left?"

I wanted to say that I am not a thief and wouldn't hurt anyone. Instead, I said a silent prayer and answered each question looking them in their eyes. My feelings were almost getting the better of me and it showed as my English reverted back to the days before my lessons with Dr. Nott:

"I ain't take nothin' 'cept food my ma made and giv' me. I dinna hurt no one, nobody. Ne'er hav', ne'er will."

Dr. Nott gave me a look, not of pride by what I said, but a caring look that caused my cheeks to get hot. I don't know if this hotness had to do with my realizing that Dr. Nott was a man with a good heart or my frustration with why they were asking these questions.

Chapter Five

The Fugitive Slave Act of 1850

Mr. Potter finished tellin' us about his journey and how he couldn't bargain down the price. Then Judge Campbell began to explain the real reason for the Fugitive Slave Act. The elder Judge sat back in his seat as he proudly began to lecture:

"The Fugitive Slave Act was established in 1850 to bring a compromise to the Southern politicians who believed in the idea and rights of slave owners, slavery, and slave states. The goal of the government was to keep the union of the States whole, while acquiring more land to the west. While new lands and territories began to join the country, the concept of slavery and slave trade in those territories became a major focus. Those against slavery wanted western states to remain free, while those for slavery did not want more pressure for slavery to end and preferred the new states of the Union to be slave states. As part of the compromise, Washington City, one of the more popular locations for slave trade was to remain a district that held slavery, but could no longer offer slave auctions and trade. So, you could own a slave, but you couldn't buy or sell a slave in this area any more. California, which is now populated due to the gold rush, would be a free state. To offset this imbalance of adding another free state, the Fugitive Slave Act was designed. Escaped slaves were considered fugitives and, therefore, if found, they would be returned to their rightful owners even if they were found in free states".

The much younger Attorney Brown was eager to pipe in and said with agitation:

"This compromise put fear and anger in the free and escaped slaves. Many Northern coloreds were also concerned because some of them who had received freedom had no papers or proof that they were no longer slaves. Other free coloreds who had never been slaves could be purposely or mistakenly kidnapped and brought to plantations as slaves. It is known that some free coloreds from the North were captured or tricked and kidnapped and brought to the South to be sold into slavery. Others, escaped or former slaves, began moving north to Canada for fear that they would be returned back into slavery. White citizens were expected to help identify escaped slaves and sometimes were paid a fee or rewarded if they assisted with a capture. Other whites were told they could be arrested for harboring escaped slaves. I believe that this law goes against all moral principles."

Dr. Nott and I knew that my safety was in jeopardy. If not a local citizen, a member of the Union College community could easily turn me in. They suggested that I needed to continue my journey north to Canada, if only for a little while, until my freedom was acquired. Dr. Nott began sharing his frustrations in a stern but deliberate tone:

"No one should pay any amount for a human being. We are all men and free under the eyes of God and therefore no one man should own another man. We are neither pets nor property."

Dr. Nott was willing to pay a reasonable price, not for me, but for my freedom. He made that statement more than once to make sure everyone understood what he was doing. But the judge and attorney stated, repeatedly that I was not safe here in Schenectady—my former master knew my location and could legally claim me at any time. Dr. Nott would be breaking the law if he continued to keep me employed knowing that I was an escaped slave. In addition, we were concerned for Dr. Nott. The judge said with annoyance:

"There could be positive and negative notoriety if he were caught harboring an escaped slave. Although located in New York, a free state, Union College has a large number of boys from the South. These students did not appreciate the antislavery discussions on campus. Southern students would support the return of an escaped slave to his owner because of the law."

That's when I realized that the parents of these southern boys would prefer that I be returned to slavery, and if I were not, they could threaten to pull their sons out of school. The college depended on their money to help pay for the faculty's salaries.

There were signs on our campus about our Southern boys' interests and Northern boys' concerns. Dr. Nott and I were noticing a number of Confederate newspapers in the boys' area so there must be some boys who would not want me around. Our library holds one copy of the Watch Tower Confederate paper for students and maybe some faculty who are particular to

Southern ideas. We did notice that the Southern students did not voice their opinion for fear of anger from Northern students, so these newspapers were read in secrecy. The Abolitionist papers were more popular on campus and read in public—the most popular being the North Star, a paper produced right here in New York.

While Dr. Nott could be arrested for harboring me in his home, he was agitated because he felt he was obeying the higher law. He stood up and quoted from the Bible, flipping through it so fast he almost tore the pages. He preached, "Galatians chapter three, verses twenty-seven to twenty eight says:

"For as many of you as were baptized into Christ have put on Christ. There is neither Jew nor Greek; there is neither slave nor free; there is neither male nor female. For you are all one in Jesus Christ." He then flipped the pages again and read from Philemon, verses fifteen and sixteen, "For perhaps she has departed for a while for this purpose that you might receive Him forever. No longer as a slave but more than a slave, a beloved brother, especially to me. But how much more to me in the flesh and in the Lord." I kept those words in my heart, "No longer a slave, but more than a slave, a beloved brother especially to me."

I think he picked this Bible verse especially for me—to understand him.

I know that Dr. Nott's views on slavery were formed in his younger years as a religious man. This is why he no longer owned the slaves he inherited from his family and spoke of the problems of slave states. At the end of the meeting, they all agreed that I needed to head north to Canada in order to keep my freedom. Dr. Nott clarified:

"Canada did not recognize the State of Slavery, nor the law that any man can be the proprietor of another".

I would only need to stay there until a deal was made between Dr. Nott and Master Murphy. The final decision was that Dr. Nott would send his grandson to Maryland to cut a deal with Murphy while I would be sent north to a little farm in Canada, to a friend of Dr. Nott. As everyone stood up, I sat there saying nothing; the decision has been made.

They decided to send me by train to the Palemont family in Canada for my safety. Dr. Nott counseled:

"We should not disclose the location of the city in Canada for fear of Moses being kidnapped and brought back into slavery. All written correspondence will transpire by me, and only to the Palemonts."

Though I had saved up some money, Dr. Nott gave me ample dollars to use for living purposes. In his generosity, he also drafted me a letter of introduction to the local bank that I was surprised to receive. It stated:

"Moses Viney is a man of great integrity, industry and capability. He is a moral and religious man in whom entire confidence can be placed. Should the funds he has taken not be sufficient, he is hereby authorized to draw on my account at the Mohawk Bank at Schenectady for any sum not exceeding one hundred dollars and I will honor the draft. Eliphalet Nott."

I planned on not using this note and making my own means to live on for what we perceived would be a short period of time, because I am already indebted to Dr. Nott's generosity. When I realized that my stay in Canada might mean it could be a few months before I would get back to my sweetheart Anna, my wife of almost one year, I decided to go for a walk in Schenectady. I walked west towards the train station downtown, just thinking and walking. I realized that I was agreeing to head north, but the anxiety I felt running for my freedom in the 1840s returned as I took in the odor of a train's steam fumes, the scents of the river and the smells of swamps. This river water smell is bittersweet and it accosts my nose. What is more troublesome is what I must now do. It hurts because I have to flee once again, first from Maryland now from Schenectady. When will I be able to stop running. And once again, I must watch over my shoulder until I successfully pass the border.

With the decision made, that evening Dr. Nott called me into his bedroom for what I thought was our usual talk while I massaged him. Now that it was just the two of us, he instead wanted to hear my story, my escape story, and he wanted to know if I had done anything illegal on the way north that might come back on me if I was free. He was concerned that I might not have wanted to share anything bad in front of anyone else. I had never really told anyone the whole story, Anna knew bits, but I wouldn't want to worry her. Dr. Nott's voice stirred me from my thoughts as I began massaging his arms, hands and fingers:

"With the talk of war going on, my son, I am now feeling that all men in this country will soon be free. Your freedom will be granted to you as well. So we are now at a time when I can hear your full story of escape before you head north. I know some people had to do bad things in order for their escape to be successful. In addition, we needed to keep the stories of escapes secret in order to help others escape. I didn't want to ask you for fear that you would tell me something and I might have to act on it. Now is the time for us to have that difficult story shared. If you feel you can't share it, I respect your stand. But also know that if you tell me, I will not share the information with others."

As he said this, I felt the tightness loosen where he was squeezing my hand. I leaned forward, still holding his hand, and as I squeezed his hands and loosened them, I stood up and placed a chair directly in front of his bed. I moved the liniment for his legs closer to my chair and I sat down and took a deep breath.

"Dr. Nott, this is a story that is so difficult to share that I haven't even told Anna the full story. It's not for fear of betraying others. No one else can be hurt in my tellin' of the story. I don't know where my two friends went off to after I left the Fonda farm. Except to say one is now west of here, and the last I saw, the other was east of here saying he wanted to go back to his motherland, Africa. It's just a difficult story to tell, but I'll tell you. I'll tell you."

And so I began my story.

Chapter Six

Escape

As I talked to President Nott, I rubbed his legs and I looked up at him and he had his eyes closed. It was easier to talk with his eyes closed even though I knew he was awake and listening.

"I planned to escape, as you know, because I knew the young Master Murphy was about to sell some of us. I didn't want to be sold away from my family and it was a time where most slave traders took slaves to the deep South. I knew Master Murphy had to sell us. It wasn't his fault. They were losing business, but I knew this was my chance to find freedom and not just go off without a fight. So I began planning about one year before the escape. I knew I needed money. I also knew that Murphy would come after me, so I had to plan a way that took into account his hunting sense."

As I recalled my past, vivid images, scents and hurts surfaced. I was talking to Dr. Nott, but it was as if I was remembering the details for myself, sharing them with myself—never pausing to discuss anything as I started to relive being on the plantation.

Living on the plantation was at times pleasant and at other times grueling and stifling. All of us slaves knew what was expected of us and would work hard to please the master and his family. Working for the senior Master Murphy in the big house was better than working in the fields. As a child, I didn't work at all. I played with his son, you know, Richard Murphy, inside the kitchen and outside in the dirt yard until I was around five years old. Master… uh, Richard and I would play all day into the night—collecting frogs, chasing balls. And he would teach me some things he learned from his schooling by his mother—reading and writing, but it was not much. My ma was the housemaid and his mammy, and I loved staying around the house to be near to her.

I am the eldest child of Horace Thomas Viney, who the elder William Murphy had bought at an auction in Baltimore. Master Murphy recorded all of the slaves' births and deaths. That's why I know my day of birth. This was not typical. Some slave owners did this to keep track of their property. Today, I have twenty-three brothers and sisters. Master Murphy was different 'cause he tried to keep slave families together. My pa and ma lived together in slave quarters. This did not mean they had separate rooms; we had one large slave cabin. We lived with one room and one wall; we lived and ate on one side of the wall and slept on the other side.

We slept on the floor, but the master was kind enough to give us a few rough but warm blankets for the dirt floors during the cold nights. There was a small loft up the ladder, where my parents slept, but the tin roof was so hot that in the summer they slept with us. The floor was cooler for all of us in the summer and our bodies kept us warm in the winter. Although we had dirt floors, we had a table and two chairs for Ma and Pa, pots and pans for cooking and cleaning, bowls for eating and hay and blankets for sleeping.

For my escape, I picked two friends to come with me and was particular to the ones who would be as desperate as me, but also would be smart to have on the journey. One had tried to escape from another plantation and the other was a strong boy from my childhood who I felt close to but who I also knew had a family that didn't treat him right. He'd run and never look back. My childhood friend was the first person I told that I wanted to run away. His family was hard on him; I don't really think they liked him, always putting him down.

He was quiet, strong but also wanted freedom as much from the slave master as he wanted freedom from his relations. I didn't know I'd have a second person until I met the escaped slave. He was smart and only got caught because of the natural elements that were against him. I felt it would be good to have someone who had tried escaping at least once. He'd be more determined to be successful the second time around.

My two friends who ran away with me were Hinson Piney and Washington Brooks. About one year before our escape, Hinson had been bought by senior Master Murphy and after a few weeks, released from shackles. He came without family and had escaped once before that my master didn't know about, which is why he had been put up for sale. Hinson spoke of being used as the whipping boy to show all the other slaves what would happen if you tried to escape. They kept him on for about a year and he worked hard hoping this would stop the beatings. Instead, they took him away from his ma and pa, since his real pa was said to be the master, and sold him. His slave pa, though living on the same plantation, had been separated from his ma, since she could not be the true wife to her husband if she was forced to bed with her master.

Hinson's master worked with a slave trader or what we called the soul driver. This soul driver bargained with Master to fetch a good sum of money for Hinson's good youth, health and light skin. Many folks say those were a sign that a slave was smarter and less lazy than dark-skinned colored. I never saw any difference, but the white man says there is a difference.

Hinson's first master did not share with Master Murphy that he had been an escaped slave for fear that he would not want to buy him. Most escaped slaves were re-sold after an escape to the deep South, territory where it was more difficult to find freedom. You only need to look at the markings on Hinson's back to know he was not a well-behaved slave. He had been beaten with the Negro whip.

All slaves were in fear of this whip which the overseer would use. Its handle was two to three feet long and sometimes the butt of it was filled with lead to make it heavier. The lash of the whip was six feet long and made of cow hide and sometimes had plaited wire at the end of it which could rip and tear at the skin. When he arrived, Master Murphy kept Hinson in shackles longer than the other slaves he had bought that spring. Hinson would share with me stories of his few days of freedom. Though he was never really free, he had made it from Bucktown to Denton, Maryland—almost sixty miles of freedom.

Hinson talked of running until his feet were bleeding and hiding in a cool cave or under leaves during the hot roasting day. He talked of the sun and moon as if they were traveling with him. He said they kept him moving north and at times he would talk to them and ask for a little less heat or more moonlight so he could see the shapes of the trees, rocks and paths. Traveling in the safety of the night moon, across marshes, worrying only about snakes and wild dogs, Hinson was caught as he was crossing under a bridge at dusk. He had not realized that he was casting a shadow as he waded in the water. While on the bridge, a lone man was watching him. Hinson had told his story to us in a soft voice:

"I was trying to cross the water under the bridge but lost footing and was quickly taken down river. I could not swim, so I kept going up and down in the water to try to catch more air. My head and face would go under and I'd come up when my chest was about to burst—grabbing air and trying to grab on to anything, a branch or stone. The lone man was running towards me on the bank and he watched as I went underwater two or three times. He was a white man and he did not try to help me. I was carried by the water towards some side brush and got caught in the branches. The man watched as I fought to keep my head above water, and he came over to watch me drown."

Hinson knew he would die a wicked death and yelled to the man to help him. Hinson said, breathing hard, with closed hands and his head down:

"The man handed me the butt of his gun to grab. I was pulled to the ground, wheezing and hacking with my face in the mud. Then, he turned me over, when I looked up, the man had his gun pointed to my heart. I licked my lips, which tasted like sweet clay, and I wondered if this would be my last meal. I did not know if I was shaking with fear from drownin' or from the point of the gun hard on my chest. I knew my taste of freedom was over. I was sad when I found out later that I had not even made it out of Maryland."

Hinson's head was now lowered to the ground. Listening to this strong boy, I wanted to be friends with him, he was a man who at least had tried to escape. Once you've tasted a moment of freedom you have a hankering for that flavor again. I would need Hinson's insight because he had seen more of the world than I and he knew how to listen to the earth, the sun, and the moon to find the way to freedom.

I had known my friend Washington since his birth. He was four years younger than I was. Washington's aunt, uncle, and father raised him on the Murphy's plantation and they were all field hands. Washington's mother died while giving birth to him or as he says:

"I killed my mother for I was too big and my small mother could not handle my size."

It was a story he had heard many times from his aunt and uncle and that I had heard many times from other slaves. Washington was a very quiet, sensitive soul but was also very perceptive. He was big for his age, over six feet tall with broad shoulders and strong arms. He was always asking questions and many times would immediately answer the question himself to his liking. After one of his responses, his chuckles would echo for quite some time and his large frame heaved, quite pleased with himself. Most folks liked his answers and would inquire more about the topic.

One day when we were talking about our escape plan, in typical fashion he asked and answered his own questions. Washington asked:

"How do you know which state is which before you leave one and get to the other? Are the areas marked with fences like the plantation? I think not. I think you just keep on a walkin' until someone tells you where you are!"

When Hinson was telling us 'bout using the sky to find north, Washington wondered:

"How can the sky hold up all the stars?" And he answered himself, "The sky does not hold up the stars. The stars hold up the sky and slowly lets go so that the morning sun could shine once more."

He added that he understood why the wise men followed the stars' brilliance and not the heat of the sun for "the stars knew when it was time to go and the sun was dependent on the stars to leave." If I was to escape, I would need Washington's insight because he had the smarts to question his surroundings and able to have the answers for safe passage.

Washington and I sort of grew up together on the plantation. Although my ma was the house slave, and my pa worked the fields, pa was seen as wise. Many people went to him for advice for ailments and such. Washington's pa was always seeking my Pa's advice. Since I grew up mainly in the big house, I would see

Washington heading to the fields in the dawn. I saw him first as a babe on his aunt's backside and as he grew older in the fields pulling tobacco. He seemed to be too young to be in the fields since he had older cousins who were still housed in slave quarters, but they made him go 'cause he was big. They always seemed to not like him 'cause he killed his mother. That's why I liked him, 'cause I didn't think it was his fault he killed her.

Washington was also in fear of being caught, beaten, resold or killed. He had seen the tracking on Hinson's back—scars so thick they formed ridges—deep, dark grooves that caused his skin to tighten at the edges and the tautness of the scarring caused the good skin on his back to have a smooth shine. Hinson also walked with his back more curved. Hinson recounted:

"The heat of the sun would sometimes cause my back to sting and burn. Salty sweat and heat ain't no good and reminds me of the whip."

Washington had heard horrible stories of those who had escaped and were caught. Some were brought back to their master's plantation and were purposely beaten to unconsciousness to set the example to other slaves. While in a deep sleep, the slaves were rudely awakened by their tormentors and doused in salted water. This caused them to scream due to the burning sting on the raw open wounds, only to be beaten again.

This ritual of being repeatedly beaten would sometimes be continued until nightfall or until their death, whichever came first. I've not seen many whippins', but sometimes I felt like the overseer received pleasure in the whipping of a slave and sometimes I felt guilty because I was relieved it wasn't me. Often the goal was to induce a slow, painful death of the slave. There were other times when the masters had gone too far not expecting the slave to die and felt they wasted money. And all of this always was done in front of the other slaves, including their family relations.

Washington would not want his family to see him beaten like this. And it would be hard on other slaves who might consider escaping in the future, to see him caught and returned and witness his demise. He would not want to block their dream of escaping to freedom. He also knew that if he was caught and returned, some of the slaves would feel envious of his escape and would then feel disappointed upon his being caught. Other slaves would chastise him for considering the stupidity of trying to escape. They'd say:

"What's up north? As slaves we now get food and shelter. How would we eat and sleep moving up north—especially because Master Murphy treated us slaves better than other masters?"

Some slaves might be angry with an escaped slave because when a master finds out that a slave has escaped, they sometimes would beat other slaves to find information on the escape plans. Smart slaves considering escape never told other slaves of their plans. Washington knew that if he did plan to escape, he could not even tell his family, for fear of them informing on him. He did not trust them for they were, and rightly so, still angry that he, due to his birth, had taken the breath away from his aunt's sister and his father's wife.

Chapter Seven

Making Plans, Facing Risks

On the Southern plantation, the work was hard and grueling, back breaking in the heat with little rest. We were good slaves, good people—doing what our master, Senior Mr. Murphy, asked us to do and many times doing more. In the winter, we slowed down but picked up at first spring. I never had to experience being sold and shackled. I got whipped only a few times as a child and learned how to avoid antagonizing the white handlers. I was told that I was to be trained as a butler—my ma might have suggested this—so I was glad to be around the house helping and learning from the house hands.

I had better clothes and I learned new words in the house, but most 'specially I sometimes slept later in the day than the field hands, though Ma was always up before the rooster crowed. Housework that I was doing was easier than the fieldwork that the slaves had to do.

Indoors as butler, the housemaids respected me. I had a duty to my master to please him, his family and his guests. I learned from them and when they used new words, I'd try using the same words. There was a bit of dignity in the position and I worked with dignity to do the best job I could. I did not realize at this time that feeling proud of a job well done was a gift of freedom and reward.

Initially, as a young'un in the house, during my free time or Sundays, I would play with the Murphy's dogs and teach them to fetch, lie down, and return back to their kennel. I was expected to learn the correct way to clean around the house by watching and helping the house servants do their work. I also learned some reading and writing from junior Murphy before he went off to school when he was a young'un. But I knew that my master didn't want us to learn and tried to keep us ignorant. I picked up a lot of words from my master's family. Sometimes I ain't used them right, but I tried to use them as much as I could.

As I learned to serve with skill and manage the household, I was trusted to bring messages to other white families and visit relatives at local farms. I would travel along the Choptank River edge, stepping with a brisk pace for two reasons: to get the messages to the families in a reasonable amount of time and because being barefoot while stepping on the prickly gumball fruit of the sweet gum trees made you want to move fast.

Slaves were not given shoes for fear of escape. One winter, I walked barefoot on the bitter, cold ground. My feet were cracked and bleeding when I got home and I could hardly walk the next day. To my surprise, my master was generous enough to give me a pair of his son's shoes which I kept until my feet outgrew them.

I could make money two ways, bringing letters to white families for pennies and stacking sheaves for the field handlers. I saved my earnings since there was rarely a time I could spend the money. Then one year, when I was about seventeen, my master died a slow, painful death which took almost two years before he met his Maker. When he died, the land and all its property went to his eldest son, but during those two years no one was watching the business of the farm. We all mourned the loss of senior Master Murphy. He was a good man, wanting to keep slave families together because he felt we worked better that way. He also only beat you when you deserved it for not working hard enough or trying to escape—or if it seemed like you were thinking about escaping.

We were all concerned now that senior Master Murphy was dead. Junior Master Murphy was different from his pa. He spent money unwisely, his ma would say in front of the house slaves. Junior Murphy had another flaw. He had an anger streak since he was a young boy. He was chubbier than most kids and I heard he was teased a lot at school. When a slave was unruly, he used the whip and his power to make himself feel good, you could tell by the look on his face, but I think it never seemed to make him feel better about himself.

Most times he had the overseer beat the slaves. It was difficult for a slave father to watch someone beat his wife or see a slave mother cry and scream to stop the beating of their child. These beatings of slaves increased as junior Master Murphy struggled with the finances. After senior Murphy's death, it was likely that junior Master Murphy would sell most of us slaves. Junior Murphy said his pa didn't do the books right the last years he was on earth. The plantation was losing money 'cause of poor fields and lack of water.

At this time, I was almost eighteen and could fetch a lot of money on the auction block. Master was greedy for gain. I was scared and worried that I would be sold. Not only would I be taken away from my family, I could be working as a field hand and even worse I could be working for a more brutal master. I decided I had to run away, escape north and find freedom before I was sold.

Chapter Eight

The Underground Railroad, Abolitionists, and the Way North

There were some things I had learned from others about escaping. If you plan to escape, don't get caught. It's better to be dead than to be caught and be a whippin' boy for the master. Getting caught could easily lead to a slow, painful death. If you plan to escape, don't tell anyone your plans except for the people who are leaving with you and make sure you know where you will go onto from that location.

People had learned about the plans that the Underground Railroad offered like hiding in the dark, following the North Star, crossing rivers so that dogs would have a hard time finding your scent, having money to buy food or to bribe others, and toughening your feet so they would not hurt while stepping on the ground on things like the stickles of the sweet gum trees.

We also knew there were white people who would help you escape; they would hide and feed you. They were called abolitionists. I was not sure how you could tell them from other white people, nor how to find them, but I was glad to know they were out there to help us escape. I decided to leave when I could have the most time to get away before being missed by the junior Master Murphy.

Before leaving, I thought about three things: having enough money once I crossed into the free states, how to find the conductors of the Underground Railroad since it was such a secret, and how to escape from the dogs who will surely know my scent that will lead to my trail. Getting the money was easy; I worked stacking sheaves and hid the money in my Liberty Fund—my pa liked that name for it.

He was the only one who knew I was planning something, but I didn't give him any details 'cause I didn't want Murphy to go after him when I was gone. Wasn't much money, but each pence brought me closer to freedom. In my head I pictured being shackled with my family. Every time I put a pence in my fund, one shackle got unlocked and dropped to the ground.

Though I was small, I was fast and the exercise of stacking put muscles on me too. I would stack sheaves fast and high as I hummed songs my ma taught me. The faster we stacked, the more we were given cents for our pockets. I put this Liberty Fund money in a box and buried it in the ground near where I slept. I did not have to think much about the Underground Railroad until I got to Denton.

I knew there were abolitionists leading an Underground Railroad there, though I didn't know how to meet it. Hinson talked of using steamboats, hiding in white men's homes and free men's churches. I would not worry about this until I was sure clear of having to keep running. Hinson also said our first stop on the freedom trail would be Philadelphia, a city where many former slaves escaped in order to continue to find the way north. He knew of a man there who could help us.

My fear of the dogs chasing me was different. I have seen junior Master Murphy handle the dogs with such fierceness and anger. These large hound dogs were ferocious when he was near. He fed them pig slop mixed with gunpowder to toughen them up. He'd hit them when he thought they lost the scent of a fallen duck or yell at them in such a gruff voice that some of the dogs whimpered. I also knew that when junior Murphy would find out about a slave escape, the first thing he would do would be to send out the dogs. So I had to figure out how to get around the dogs.

They were good hound dogs, smart and eager to please. It wasn't necessary to abuse them to get them to obey. Junior Master Murphy chose to have a heavy hand towards them and they feared him. It must have been another way for the master to make himself feel better. In contrast, I began to first play with the dogs and then train them. I would give the dogs table bits for rewards if they did what I said. Junior Murphy gave them whippings or yelled at them when they didn't obey.

I got the dogs to come and go as I signaled. Most of my signals were sounds, a clap, a whistle, a movement with my hands. I'd have to handle the dogs in a way that they would obey me despite their fear of our master.

Every day I began to feed the dogs and play with them a bit more. As they got more and more comfortable with me, I would give them a bit of good table food when they obeyed my commands. I would also give them a sweet snack when they were scolded by our master. Yes, "our master," both dogs and slaves, were property of the masters. As I moved the dogs around the plantation, I said commands like, "Go home," and I'd watch them head back to their shack to eagerly await my return and snack. I'd move further away, giving them the command but also not rewarding them with a snack for a few hours until I returned; they would wait patiently for me. Then I would give them a larger quantity of reward. When I could get all of the dogs to go back to their shacks without fear and to patiently wait there until I returned, I knew I would be ready for my escape. I continued to train the dogs as I thought about the right day to leave.

We needed to pick a day when we would not be noticed for quite some time. As you know, even around here we have the Easter Sunday holiday. Well, we slaves were given time to visit other relatives in the next county. Easter was a few months away and the master allowed slaves he trusted to visit their families in other parts of the county. There was an Easter festival in the next town. This holiday always gave us two days off, Easter Sabbath Sunday and Monday.

If we left early Sunday for the festival, we would not be noticed until after midday on Monday. Although junior Master Murphy was uncomfortable with the travel of the most recent slave of the three of us, Tom, I said I'd watch over him. Master allowed us to head out for Easter festival, visit family, and return by the noon hour on Monday.

Junior Master Murphy entrusting me with both men to go visit relatives and to return the next day was an answer to the prayer of righteous men. The only thing I regret is that I gave him my word to watch over the other two slaves. It took me awhile to get over the guilt of breaking the trust, but as I see it, I didn't go back on my word. Instead, his idea of "watch over" and my idea of "watch over" were two different ideas. The situation in my telling this still troubled me so much that I was aware of Dr. Nott's presence again. I looked up at him. Dr. Nott was enjoying the massage as much as the story, and he nodded and just said, "I can see that many people have the notion that what they mean is the same as what another person means. The good Lord understands your idea of 'watch over'." I inhale deeply, feeling good that Dr. Nott appreciates my interpretation. I continue the story and withdraw back into my past.

I, now, thank God for the opportunities I found to earn my own money. As I said, stacking the sheaves not only gave me money for my Liberty Fund, it also helped build my muscles. Altogether, I had saved about $20 to use for my freedom, had very little belongings and knew that if we didn't run away this Easter, we would be sold by the next. On Easter eve, I ventured to my parents' quarters and told them of my leaving.

Ma, a small woman, who seemed taller than her God-given height, had tears in her eyes. She was sturdy in her stance and held me tight and I wrapped my arms so completely around her that I thought she would disappear into my hug. She prayed in my ear for my freedom, which tickled a little. I held the memory of this tickle in my heart, her smile and the sweet smell of sleepiness on her. Pa, knowing more than Ma, said he knew this day would come. He wished he was younger to join us, but he knew with the other children and his love for my ma that he could never leave. He told me to be sure to break free so I wouldn't be sold to what might be a more Southern brutal master. He gave me a hug and whispered in my ear:

"Do not get caught, no matter what. If you are brought back here, you will live a life in evil ways."

Hinson, Washington, and I did not sleep well that night. We were too anxious to sleep, but we knew we needed to rest for our long journey. I told them what my pa had said. We embraced and vowed to each other that we would never be taken back—no matter the costs. In the morning, just like the other two housemaids, we received two biscuits and a piece of fatback for our journey to the festival. My mom tossed in a small sweet for me. As I gazed into her eyes, I realized this would be the last time we would be with each other. Before she could tear up, she flustered and began to fill up Tom's and Isaac's bags and sent us on out the door.

As I looked towards the field, the dawn still not breaking, I could see the shadow of the tall figure of my pa. I could not see his face, but the nod of his worn floppy hat on his head gave me courage for this long, dangerous, and in some ways exciting journey. I would not know the true feeling of excitement though until I was safe in the land where all are free.

Dr. Nott turned over so I could massage the other leg. He moaned when I gave it the first heavy squeeze. I continued my story.

We headed out and although we had clean clothes, we did not have shoes. Now, understand, it is rare for slaves to have shoes. I had shoes when I worked in the house— always leftover shoes from some other person—so my feet softened. But since they had to put me back in the fields, the shoes were too small and ruined. It took a while for my feet to toughen again and I knew I had to have tough feet in order to cover the ground I'd be walking, crossing river edges covered in gumball tree bristles and climbing in and out of swamp water.

That early morning before leaving for what we had said was our visit to relations, I said proper goodbyes to my ma and pa in front of some of the Murphy family. This was typical and would not draw attention to our intentions. We all left as was planned with a group of about eight of us heading to the next county. But the three of us separated from the pack.

We knew we had to run until exhaustion into the evening 'cause the master would find out first thing when the others returned. The first few miles were a breeze in the wind. We walked with the house-slaves initially but then slowly picked up pace and walked ahead. As the maids went out of our sight, we began a brisk walk-run down behind the hills and houses towards the city of Denton, Maryland. We knew we had to get to the Choptank River to follow it north towards freedom. We also knew that the master and his posse would be behind us.

We did not stop running. We found the river and followed it north, not at the edge of the river, but we followed the sound. We had to wait to cross the river at the point in Easton where it is low and narrows with a moving bridge. We'd have to do this in the dark of the night. So we kept running until dark and then we walked slowly on the clearest, darkest night with only the moon lighting the trees. We were hungry and stopped only a few minutes to eat what Ma had packed for us. That was the last time I tasted my ma's good cooking. I can still taste her biscuits on my tongue right now. Anyway, we licked the last bits off our fingers as we headed towards the moving bridge to Denton.

In reaching Denton, a seventeen-mile trek by early darkness, the river flow would be our guide. What we didn't know was whether when the house slaves got home would they be forced to share that we had gone far ahead of them and they hadn't seen us since we parted ways. They would have to go back to the plantation on their own. By the time Master Murphy would find out, we would be long gone and almost to freedom and so the hunt would begin and we knew the master would set the dogs out after us.

As we reached the moving bridge to cross into Denton, daylight was up on us. We traveled carefully across to the highest point of Choptank River and just as we were scurrying north we saw and heard a lot of people. We looked up and there were people on the Court House Green having a picnic. We knew they saw us so we headed back across the bridge which was not the direction we needed to go. As soon as we got back across, we heard the dogs. I knew they were the bloodhounds – whose, we were not sure but we weren't waiting around to find out. They were barking and moving fast.

Hinson and Washington looked at me with fear in their eyes. I was scared too, but I decided this was my chance. I told them to run and we ran but the dogs were tracking fast and before I knew it one had me on the ground with his teeth bearing for my neck. He had foam running from the side of his jowls and anger in his eyes. And next I knew he stopped and smelled, and smelled my neck again and then he began licking my face.

These were the Master's lead dogs. I could see the bushes moving a ways down the river and the dogs heading our way while Hinson and Washington were running away. I had to get the dogs to head home. I gave the first signal, a simple whistle, and watched this lead dog step off me and cock his head, circling me in confusion. I just lay there still, then gave a second signal, a long, harder whistle with claps. He became his eager self, circled one more time as I began to stand and he started heading back in the direction from which they came. Then the other dogs began to follow the lead dog back down the river. The master's group had not caught up with them and I wasn't waiting 'round to watch. I jumped down the little hill we were on, ran back north up the river, saw that both Hinson and Washington and caught up with them.

We ran hard from there on. We now had to find another way back across the river. We were tired, dirty and scared, but we made a pact to go on no matter what. We did just that.

Dr. Nott began to stir but his eyes were wide opened. Unfortunately, I now realize that we did break one of the Ten Commandments, but I only learned about the commandments when I came North. We had to eat to stay strong. We stole a pie cooling near a window of one farm house and we stole vegetables from one garden. I regret that we stole things that may have hurt others.

Washington had also lost part of his pants somewhere along the way and they were damp. We saw a line of clothes drying on the breezy, sunny day. Now all we really needed was the pants hanging, but we were so dirty we also took three shirts. As we continued running up the edge of the river, kind of in the forest and out of the forest, we saw a small canoe. We decided we needed it more than the owners of it did, since the canoe might save our lives and was probably only used to feed the family fish who owned it. We looked around and there were no paddles so we took apart their picket fence and used the boards as paddles on the river.

We left the canoe at a bank when we thought we were safe. We thought the family should be able to find it there. Then we started running until we saw the river widening. Washington decided to stay a little away from us so if he saw someone he could ask the questions 'cause he was smart at asking questions. He found out from a young lad, who he said was a Quaker, that we were in Smyrna, Delaware. This is the port where many steamboats sailed north. Here we worried intensely due to our needing to keep our eyes open for slave catchers.

I turned to Dr. Nott and confessed:

"To this day, I feel bad for the family whose pie we took, but more for that family that had the canoe. They were poor, living off the land and the river. I don't know if they were able to retrieve the vessel. This is what I would ask forgiveness for."

Dr. Nott was nodding his head, saying:

"That's good of you 'cause you know, my boy, God doesn't like stealing. But he knows you have remorse and he is a forgiving God."

With that, I felt much better. Then Nott asked:

"Through all your travels did you find anyone along the Underground Railroad?"

I paused and looked up to him and replied:

"Hinson knew about the Railroad. He had the name of the church we needed to reach in Philadelphia. They helped us get to Troy. We did not find Harriet Tubman, the woman called Moses, like others had done, but we had some help and God was watching over us they say. We met up with some Quakers in Maryland and they told us the way."

I stretched my arms and fingers as I moved to Dr. Nott's shoulders and continued:

Hinson knew of a fellow who could get us on a steamship from Pigs Point to Philadelphia. Washington and I waited in a very dark alley. The smell of fish and boats hurt to breathe in. Hinson came running back to us and gave us each a dark cap to wear. He said the fellow needed $10, which was half the money I had in my Liberty Fund, so I reached in and pulled out $5. Hinson looked curious as I explained that I would give the man $5 more when we reached Philadelphia, the land of the free. Hinson left and a short time later returned with a smile. He said, 'That fella thinks you're a smart one and said you are going to need it when we get north.' And with that, he took the money and told me to wait here until I heard three whistles. I was terrified and expected the worst as I waited on the dock for whatever would happen next.

We are to put on our hats and file in line with the other coloreds, but to find him when we got to the inside of the ship. Washington wiped the sweat off his forehead. I'm not sure if he was hot or scared. We each put our hats on, waited for the whistle and filed in line on board and into the belly of the ship. As we reached the bottom, Hinson looked at another colored fellow and we moved to a room with fish-smelling gear and watched as he closed the door and told us to remain there until he returned.

Chapter Nine

From Maryland to Philly—and Hinson's Slave Ship Story

The ride on the ship was rocky. Not one of the three of us had ever been at sea. The rocking of the ship and water waves caused my head to hurt as if it was going to burst. We were all less nervy on the ship but illness took us fast. The seas were dark at night with only the bare light of the moon and stars, which were covered by heavy clouds. We could hear the shipmates talking through the floorboards.

It had rained all day into the night which the shipmates said caused the waves to be high, moving us back and forth. We hadn't eaten much on the run, but our throats kept heaving nothing but air on our empty bellies. We stayed in the hull of the ship as demanded by the one shipmate we met. We were sweating, holding our heads and bellies at the same time.

Hinson started talking about the ship and telling us an old story. He said our people came on ships bigger than this. I had heard these stories from my people, too. He was older and said he had stories from his grandpa. He began by saying how much worse the ship was that brought all slaves from Africa than the one we were on. He said:

"In Africa, we were free. We were kings and queens and then the white man came, bought us from our people, and chained us."

He took a deep breath, looked down at his hands and started his story in a soft voice:

"PaPa was not my real grandpa. He was the eldest slave and we all called him PaPa. He would tell us stories. He said he was only a boy in a place called Sierra Leone. One day, he was playing with his sister and their world began to change. Men from another tribe came and started shooting loud bangs.

"He had never heard these sounds before 'cause they had never seen a rifle. PaPa did not know what a gun was. It was just loud noise that he had never heard before. The sound sent the birds, and all the animals screaming away. These tribesmen were not from PaPa's tribe and they rushed into the tribe with very white men. One of the men took out a gun, which looked like a large tree branch and out came smoke and a loud noise. When PaPa looked up, his uncle's hands flew up in the air and his belly was open with red water and white masses of his insides coming out of him.

"He didn't call it blood. His uncle fell hard on his back. His people stopped 'cause they never saw anything like it. Uncle's spirit went up in the sky. Our world had come to an end."

Hinson took another breath and said in a more angry voice, "PaPa said that other white men came running with whips and beat everyone, his mom, his sister. His father tried to fight them off so he began punching and kicking, but they beat them so bad."

Hinson told us what PaPa said in his words.

"I was lost from my people, my family. I was chained with four others by our ankles and wrists. They were from my tribe, but not my family. Remember, we were not slaves until we were forced to come here to America. We walked for over three nightfalls to the edge of the earth, to the sandy dirt and blue waters with little food. If we fell while walking, we were beat across our backside with a whip. We were put on a small shell boat where people with big sticks pushed the waters 'til we got to a very large ship. If you stayed quiet as a tortoise, you didn't get beat, so I stopped fighting and stopped talking. I said nothing—no words in my head, nothing in my heart. I did not know where my family was. I was scared."

Hinson was a good storyteller. He continued in PaPa's words.

"We were on the ship for many a moon. We were laid together, could not stand for the floor was only a few hands to the head. We crawled around for we could not fully stand. Sleeping in our mess sometimes we moaned. We did not get much food and what we got was mush and soft. People got sick, so much sickness. If they fell into eternal sleep they were pushed off the ship. We had to carry them from beneath the belly of the ship.

"We would argue to help carry, for it was the only time we saw sun, stars, and breathed good air. As we carried people, the women would moan a slow, deep, painful sound and sob into their chests. We knew that some who we carried were not yet on the other side; they would be moaning and alive but they were pushed off the ship into the dark waters. Some didn't fight, they sank fast. Others fought with their arms, but went under quickly. And we would then be struck on our backs as they rushed us down to the belly of the ship."

Selling Slaves on Blocks

Hinson paused for a moment, then said, "When we came to this new land, we were hurrying to get off. When they took us off the ship, the sunlight blinded us and burnt our eyes. We were marched to a large hut. They poured cold water over us, which felt good, so we washed for the first time in the many moons that had passed since being in our home.

"Then, they put us up on blocks with our hands still bound. We did not know this new tongue; these people talked too low and too long in their words. We were placed on a block of wood, some wearing rags, some not wearing anything. White people looked us up to our heads and down to our feet, opened our mouths and put their hands in counting teeth. We dared not bite out of fear. They made us turn around and saw our backsides. White men waved their hands and yelled—those that yelled the loudest got one of us and we boarded their cart shackled together.

"Babies cried when their mothers were taken away from them. Mothers cried when their babies were taken away from them— some of these babes were still suckling."

Hinson continued to tell his story and though he was looking at us, when our eyes met I thought he was in a trance as he relayed such suffering, kind of looking through us:

"PaPa said, 'I had never seen men so white with big mean grins and I was in fear of them. And for a moment, just a moment, I saw the slow walk of my ma. It was her, shackled to another person—no clothes on. I know my ma was ashamed. She had been a princess. She was a good woman; she is still a good woman. Those white men did not know my ma. I was so happy to see my ma that I yelled for her.

'She screamed for me, but those white men turned around and they beat her back and she fell to the ground. I was smacked on the head so hard the brightness flicked off and on and I was pushed forward. I got my wits and tried to find her in the crowd, but was never to see my mother or anyone of my relations again.' "

As Hinson told this story we sat quietly, no more heaving from our guts, no more complaining.

Some talked of Moses coming to take us and free us. We had a song about Moses, which they say was from the Bible, that I remember so we started humming it together.

> *Go Down Moses*
> *Way down in Egypt land*
> *Tell Ole' Pharaoh*
> *To let my people go*
> *When Israel was in Egypt land*
> *Let my people go*

Oppressed so hard they could not stand
Let my people go
"Thus spoke the Lord," bold Moses said
Let my people go
"If not I'll smite your first born dead."
Let my people go.

Hinson said he liked this song we were humming 'cause Egypt is in Africa he said. As my mind wandered as we sat there in silence, suddenly we felt the ship hit a bump and we fell over in surprise. We heard a lot of talking and yelling above us. We could see through the wall cracks—white and colored people moving and shoving things. We waited until the shipman came down to us. He told us to wait until it got completely quiet and he would come back to get us.

We waited. It seemed like a long wait, but the sounds from above calmed down after the ship stopped rocking. Then we bumped into something. We waited for a while and then the shipmate came back and held out his hand. I placed the other $5 in coins into his hand and as he closed it I clasped his hand. He held on and held my elbow. As we looked into each other's eyes, I knew I was about to walk on free soil.

Chapter Ten

Philadelphia, a.k.a. "Freedelphia"

We knew who we wanted to see in this city called Philadelphia and as we crept off the ship down the wooden board, we began to walk. At first, walking on solid ground felt funny 'cause it felt like the street was moving like the ship on water. But the pushing and shoving on the street had me hold my breath as I walked—to where we didn't know. It was eve and slightly dark. Only working colored folks were around looking at us, but they turned their heads away.

We were to find the Bishop Alexander Wayman at the Mother Bethel AME Church. We finally saw another lone colored boy a little ways from the ship. He came towards us slowly and we went forward in silence putting out our hands as was the usual custom. The man took my hand in his and placed his other hand on top and looked me in the eye. His eyes were filled with tears though not one dropped. I looked at him with moist eyes, not sure why I could only say the church's name, "Mother Bethel Church."

He smiled and nodded. We began to walk with him. He asked how many days we had been escaped from the South. I said many moons and it was hard on our bodies. He smiled from the corners of his mouth. We walked awhile. The people were walking fast through muddy streets with houses too close together, buildings taller than our highest trees, different clothes these colored people wore, and everyone except the children had on shoes. We walked, excited and exhausted, then stopped in front of the most beautiful, tall building on the street. A group of colored people walked down the white stone steps, women wearing big hats and children with socks and shoes. We walked up the most brilliant white stone stairs as if going to a better place of glory.

As we entered, we saw rows and rows of long chairs as if more than one person could sit on them, or one very large man. He pointed towards a door. We are quickly taken downstairs. As we reached the bottom, a very soft-faced, round woman met us. The man who brought us downstairs said: "You are free."

I looked at him long and hard as I tasted the salty tears on my lips. I looked at Hinson and Washington. Hinson was sitting on the steps sobbing into his hands. Washington was just standing with his eyes closed.

I looked over to the woman who had a smile like my ma. I don't remember my mother smiling very often, but when she did, she was beautiful. She said, "I am Hattie, welcome to freedom. I will take care of you.' Hattie was a lovely name, a comfortable name. She drew out a big metal pan—bigger than the pig slop on the farm—and poured water into it.

She said, "This is your first stop in freeland. You will bathe and I will get you some clothes before you meet the Reverend."

She quickly left the room. This surprised me 'cause on the plantation, a woman of her age would not care about who sees who.

Each of us in turn stepped into the water and washed our whole bodies, from our toes to our ears with a bar of soap, something that I had only seen in the master's house. We even scrubbed our hair. The soap felt smooth, though it stung us where we had cuts we hadn't noticed on our feet, arms and legs from our escape in the woods. We each had a turn and dried off with towels left for us. We did this quietly and eventually sat in silence, towels wrapped around our waists.

Hattie came back with piles of clothes she put on the table. We held up the clothes, each choosing for the right size. We put on the clothes which were the finest in the land. After we dressed, she finally peeked in and then stopped as she looked at our feet. She said, "All will know you have escaped because you have nothing on your feet. We must see how big your feet are to get you the right shoes."

She made us sit and took to placing a string from our heels to our toes. She did this for each of us and then she left. We looked at each other in amazement. Washington said, "Did she say shoes? Not real shoes like the master wears? Only house slaves wear shoes."

He said, with surprise and wonder as he and Hinson looked at me. They knew that when I was a butler I had worn shoes. She came back in with three of the most blackest, shiniest shoes. We all sat down on the floor. She gave each of us a pair.

I looked at my shoes. The back was big, the front was round, the buttons were small. These were nearly new. I never had shoes like this. My friends had never worn shoes 'cause they were field hands, but I was a house boy and had hand-down shoes from the Murphy family home. I only had shoes that were old, worn. Most of my shoes leaned over wrong and were too big or too small. I never had almost new shoes. I slipped the first shoe on and felt the leather tighten on my feet. My toes were pushed together, but the bottom was smooth and cool.

As I put the other one on, I looked up at Washington. He was slowly putting on one shoe and as he did, he gave a big sigh, put his head down and his shoulders slumped. I knew he was taking a moment for himself. I stood up on these tight hard shoes and, as I stood, I almost tilted over, which caused Hinson and Hattie to giggle. Washington looked up and started to laugh, too, chuckling like he used to from time to time. Now he could delight in so much more.

I took one to two steps and realized I had to learn to walk all over again. The shoes were heavy and hard on the floor. I picked up these heavy weights on my feet, placing one foot in front of the other—knee up and down. My friends continued to laugh as they got up off the floor and tried to walk in their shoes, stumbling like mules in mud.

Although I was the best at it, we all walked around with heavy steps, holding the walls at times until we were steady on our feet. Hattie was at the front door, smiling and pleased. I, on the other hand, was thinking that if we had to run again, the first things I'd take off were these shoes and hoped not to leave them behind. Hattie was now standing at the door seeming to block us from leaving. She looked us in the eyes, each of us individually. I realized she was about to say something important. She opened her mouth and shut it abruptly as her cheeks got bright red and her eyes became moist. I didn't know what to do, so I lowered my eyes and looked at the floor and my new shoes, so as not to embarrass her. As I looked up, she took a small white cloth out of her sleeve, dabbed her eyes and took a deep breath.

She began to tell us, "The Lord has made a way for your freedom, for all of our freedom. Take time to remember the Lord and ask the Lord to remember you. When you are in trouble and when you are on your journey, ask the Lord to remember you."

She took us back upstairs; we must've gone up four or five flights and down a long hall to a door in the back. It was dark. She held a candle to show us the way. The door in the back was slightly opened. The flickering of the candle made it look like the door was moving and the hall was long.

She walked in and introduced us to "The Right Bishop Wayman." We all held our hands by our sides and didn't reach out our hands, since we didn't know what "the right" meant. He was sitting behind a big table with lots of papers on it. This meant he could read and maybe write. He stood almost ten hands tall and almost as wide as the desk. He was a big man who was obviously a most satisfied eater. He came around the desk and shook each of our hands with his large ones.

Chapter Eleven

The Sudden Journey from Philadelphia to New York

The Right Bishop Wayman was a deep-voiced man who kinda scared you when he talked in a loud voice:

"Freedom, men, means responsibilities. There are many people, mainly white people, who say freeing a slave would mean they'd go wild, like animals. You folks aren't animals."

He seemed to bellow and didn't wait for an answer: "You folks are young men, no longer boys, who can work hard and live a decent Christian life here in free country. You will be servant to none. Where you all come from, what state or county?"

I bowed my head to this man who seemed like a king and said: "We are from Denton, in Maryland. We all came from the same plantation. We was told to come here to Philadelphia to be free."

And as I said this, I realized this man was saying we are truly free.

I remember one late, bright night when I couldn't sleep 'cause my Ma and Pa were moaning all night. I think they must have eaten something bad, but sometimes I heard them talking though I couldn't hear what they said. I could see the window and decided to go out on this cool evening in the start of spring. It was only last year. I had to step over my brother and around the head of another brother until I reached the door and went outside.

The stars were shining so bright and the moon was almost so full that it looked like the sun. I was startled when I heard the door squeak open again. There was my father who walked over to me. Pa was a soft-spoken man who always spoke his mind to me and the other coloreds, but never to the white man. He knew to look at the floor, not look them in the eye, and agree with any white man no matter what they say.

He once said, "Agreeing with the white man helps you live longer and duck the whip."

He came over and put his hand on my shoulder and looked up at the moon. He said, "Many a colored have looked in the sky and know they will always be a slave. Many a colored look in the sky and see a whole new place of freedom. They say freedom is in the North."

I asked him, "How do they know where north is and what is freedom?" He answered:

"See that most bright star in them skies? That's the North Star, and when you follow it at night, it takes you to freedom. But getting to freedom may cost you your life. I want, every day, for my children to be free for I will never see freedom. Freedom means going to sleep when you want after a hard day's work. Freedom means gettin' wages for work. Yes son, getting money for all that you do for your work. And freedom means knowing you will never fear havin' to watch a white man take a switch to your wife or your children. No one is allowed to do that in the free land."

My pa had only to witness his children being whipped, but not my ma. I believe my pa was whipped 'cause there are slight scars on his arms and backside.

Then he said, "Son, if anyone in the family is going to see freedom, it is you. When you are free, I want you to have a wife and many children for I want to know that I'd be the grandpa of free grandchildren. But you are not ready for freedom. You will know, and you be smart, you will one day see freedom and never get caught. I don't know if I will ever see the day, but on Earth or as spirit I will know that my children's children will be free."

I realized as he was talking, he now had his arm around my shoulder, pulling me tight, and that his eyes were wet as we looked to the sky for hope.

The Right Bishop Wayman was talking a lot now, walking around his desk, looking out the window and we sat bobbing our heads in agreement with what he was saying. And I think, I am free. I am a free man. Then I took to notice what he was saying, we won't be truly free until we head to a place called Troy, New York. He looked in our eyes one by one.

"You boys are still too close to your plantation. Your master will come after you here for they know this would be a first place for slaves. If you had come from the Carolinas or Georgia then you'd be safer here 'cause there are so many directions you could go. But from

Maryland to Pennsylvania, Philadelphia is the first city they would come looking for you. You need to go further north, You need to go to Albany, or Troy, or even Canada."

I had no idea where these places were and now I had a burning fear again in my belly. We were not safe yet; we were not yet truly free. We had to keep going further north.

And then he yelled so loud we all jumped in our skins:

"HATTIE, come on up here now, HATTIE!"

We heard Hattie come up the steps, not too fast 'cause there were lots of steps, but she burst in the door breathing hard, bent over with one hand on the desk and the other on her chest. We waited a minute or two until she stood up and softly said,

"Yes, Bishop, what's all the fussing?"

The Right Bishop Wayman stood tall and said, "We must help these young men get to New York where they will be safer. We must send them after they get a full supper and a good night's sleep and a big breakfast."

He sat us down and said he had a plan and we listened carefully to how a wagon would take us to one location and we would be told how to get to another city and how the walk would take us many moons until we would find true freedom. He told us of who we could talk to, but to always talk with a white person with our backside standing straight, and looking at their chest, but with a colored person looking at their eyes. This so that they would not think we were slaves who looked at the ground and feared the white man.

Each one of us put to memory all the stops on our journey to safer freedom. We all took our responsibility. We were not afraid because we were in free land. We just had to be wary of white men and, according to Bishop Wayman, even the colored men, figuring we were runaways and wanting to turn us in for rewards. Hattie said that with our new clothes and wearing of shoes, it would be hard for anyone to think we were escaped slaves. She knew we were leaving and made a big breakfast of grits, eggs, cornbread, fatback with gristle so salty I could have cried, and hot coffee.

This was a bitter and sweet time for the eve before; we ate a supper that a king would enjoy and met many colored people, free and escaped slaves. And now we must go and trust many others to help us get to Troy in New York—a place that seems now as far as, well, as far as the moon but with the North Star once again to guide us. Although this time we can travel in the morn, eve and in the night sky. As we continued our pursuit for freedom, we were sure that plans were being made for our capture.

As I said this, I watched Dr. Nott's head nod. He was drifting off to sleep and I let his leg down gently. I looked out the window to the moon high on the horizon and smiled. Leaving the room quietly I could hear the soft snore as Dr. Nott's pain had lessened and he was off to a deep sleep.

Chapter Twelve

Through the Young Master's Eyes

It has been so difficult since Pap died. He was sick for over two years and ran the farm into the ground. Within a year of his death, three of my slaves have run away— three of my strongest, hardworking slaves. The one slave I want returned is Moses...Moses Viney. Moses and I grew up together on my pap's plantation. I trusted him; he betrayed me. I used to teach him writin' and readin' until my Pap told me to stop. Pap said Moses was gettin' too good at it and we don't need no smart negroes. Gotta keep them working hard. He was getting too good at it almost better than me.

We treat our slaves good and Pap said they don't need no education or they get ideas. Pap had these notions how to keep slaves from escaping. We keep their family together, we feed them meat—not too many owners do this and we give them a good shed and some chairs— this keeps them happy and in good health. And now my slaves betray me and have gone and run away. Pap's dead. I have to run the plantation and they don't respect me. I hate this; I wanted to go on to college, take up somethin' that makes me some money, but I have to be here for family. Pap's death has really hurt Mother. She is so sad and barely comes down in day clothes.

I have been looking through our books and don't know how Pap could feed all the slaves and family, and field hands with the finances so bad. The slaves listened to Pap, but I've had to whip some of them 'cause they are too comfortable – that's what my friends say. They say we treat them too good and what good did that do for they run away anyway.

Pap was so proud of our plantation, our family and the fact that we never lost a slave due to runaways. Pap said 'cause of the Bible, he respected the slaves and treated the slaves right. They had food and a hard tin roof over their heads, not huts like some folks had for their slaves and Pa tried to keep families together. This way they were less likely to run away 'cause they had it good here.

My friends say they have it too good and talk about slaves wanting freedom, but they won't know what to do with freedom. After looking at the books, I know I will have to sell some slaves. What do they think, that I can't sell them – my friends say the slaves got a notion that I can't sell them, but I have to. I need to sell the strong, young male slaves and childbearing slave girls to get the most money.

Pap says it's embarrassing when slaves run away because it means that the owners treat them badly, beat them, and hurt them. I only beat them now when they need it, like when Lil' John was caught nappin' near the pigpen under the tree instead of working. I beat him but I didn't know he was sick. He deserved to be beat, lazy colored boy. How was I to know he was sick? He died the next day. I was planning to sell him and could've got $75, but he gone up and died. How is that supposed to help me?

After Pap died and with Lil' John gone—he was a good young farmhand—I had to move Moses from his butler work in the house back to the farm. He is worth too much and must be sold. Moses is hardworking and trustworthy and worth a lot of money. We were born on the same day, but have not been close since our youth. I trusted him with those slaves. I trusted him 'cause he never betrayed my father when he was a house slave.

The Bible says it is all right to own slaves, we just need to treat them right. It says it in the Bible, in the book of Leviticus I'm told:

"You may purchase male or female slaves from among the foreigners who live among you. You may treat them as your property, passing them on to your children as a permanent inheritance."

We have always treated them right, unless they were uppity. We had to whip some of them and straighten them out. We don't want slaves getting any ideas and we wanted to set an example of what could happen if you didn't mind the field hands.

When I look at the books, we are barely able to keep the farm. I look around and now realize, as Pap got older, he didn't keep up the house, the fences need whitewashing, and the harvest isn't as strong as it used to be. I should have been watching and helping Pap more, but he was in charge and I was learning at school. Upon his death, I am now burdened to keep the family together. I won't tell Mother about selling slaves; she is too close to some of them and right now she don't need no more grieving.

I sat with two slave traders a few months ago. They told me about the amount I would receive to sell some of the slaves. I was thinking I would keep slaves who do a good harvest, but I must also sell those who will fetch the most money. I will need to sell at least 8 grown men, but not old slaves. I will also need to sell 5 childbearing-age girls and also a few children. Pap would hate that I might be separating families, but I think grown men, sons of older slaves, could be sold and easily moved to another local plantation. They don't need their ma's anymore. They may be able to come back and visit. I will sell the girls but if I sell very young children, I will sell them with their ma.

I can't afford to keep some of the couples together. I have to remember. They are just property and although Pa would hate me doing it this way, I have to. We need the money. It would be easier for Mother to not know. She never goes out to the slave house. She may hear it from the house slaves, but I won't be selling any of the colored girls in the house.

And now I've lost three slaves, all of them sellable—good money gone to rubbish. My anger is at Moses. He was here the longest; he knew his place and he knew better. He used to be a good house slave, so we trusted him. He never rebelled, he was raised with me, and we shared birthdays. How could he betray me and my family? We needed him. He is worth so much more than the average slave. House slaves sell for more money—I could've fetched a lot for him, maybe $1,000. Now that he be escaped, not too many would want him and I'd have to send him to the deep South.

The day when I found out that the slaves were missing, I knew he was the leader, although that new colored boy had tried to escape before. Why did I trust them? That day when we went after those boys with the dogs, I think we were so close to finding them. It had only been one night and they couldn't have gone far. I don't understand how those stupid dogs led us in a circle back to the plantation. When I got back, I whipped them so bad I almost lost one of them hounds and he now walks with a limp. But those dogs know to obey me now.

We tried to get the other slaves to tell us what they knew about the escape. But after using one of the slaves, around the same age as the escapees, as a whipping boy, we got no information. We had to set an example with that whipping boy 'cause we did not want other slaves to run. Moses' ma and pa were just as scared to hear they were missing and his ma broke down screaming with worry and fretted about no longer seeing him and that maybe he was dead. We knew they didn't know and my mother trusted them.

Now see what Moses has done? We had to stop allowing slaves to go to other plantations. That ain't right, but we don't trust them no more. Folks had been talking about a war 'cause the North don't like our ability to own slaves. They didn't need no slaves 'cause they don't have plantations like we have in the South.

Then I had to lose face and tell the slave traders my slaves had escaped. They told me to put up posters and told me many stories of slaves being brought back by their owners. I gave up looking, but some folks said many slaves go to northern New York to try to get to

Canada. But now I'm hearing about this new Fugitive Slave Law that might come through. It says the Northerners have to return our slaves or they will go to jail.

I heard from some people that they think they seen Moses up north in New York. Those Northerners finally understand that owning slaves is our legal right; we paid for them and without them we can't run our plantations and sell our wares. We protect the slaves. They are ignorant, not educated and so we must give them food and clothes to protect them. They won't know what to do if they have freedom. What do the Northerners think is going to happen? Are they going to feed and clothe the slaves? Are they going to provide shelter? Now because of this law, they know that the slaves are ours, our property, and just like they have laws saying no one can steal their horses, and these horses must be returned to their rightful owners—no one can steal our slaves, they must be returned.

Chapter Thirteen

Freedom on the Fonda Farm

After many days of walking, finding safe people to talk to in Troy New York we decided to head west to a City called Schenect'y. We heard there was work their making brooms or on farms. We were put in touch with a man named Mr. Fonda who needed farming help and he said he would pay us. Only Washington and I worked on the Fonda Farm. Hinson had decided in Troy that he was never going to be caught again and kept heading northwest towards Syracuse with others who wanted to go to Canada. He also wanted to find a way back to Africa. Washington and I were working—employed—by Mr. Fonda as field hands.

Fieldwork on the Fonda farm in this city called Schenectady was not as grueling as in the South. We were not beaten nor watched by the white man as we worked the field. We were expected to plant, pick or pull in a certain amount of crops per day depending on the season. If we did less, we'd get paid less, if we did more, we'd get paid more. The weather was always mild with a breeze and on really hot days, the humidity was less torturing than the beaming hot Southern sun on our heads and backs.

The Fondas allowed the field hands to break for water and for meals. We were field hands, not slaves, and so we were paid, although at the beginning I worked on the farm. The Fondas realized that I was also a good hand around the house. I could fix broken items in the house, which led to me assisting the maid with indoor chores and eventually assisting guests as they arrived.

It is while doing this work that I met Dr. Eliphalet Nott. The Fondas were expecting company one day. The maid was working hard, dusting and cleaning. They didn't have a cook, so the maid also had to cook that day. Mr. Fonda was stressed because Mrs. Fonda wanted the house to look good for their company that was to be arriving at noon, but it was only early morning.

As I watched the women folk running around like a chicken with their heads chopped off, I saw Mr. Fonda in his study pulling out his favorite cigars to be placed on the desk and being very jittery. I went in and asked was there anything I could do to help the situation. He looked up at me from his big desk and chair and said, "You all we need to put on airs 'cause the President of Union College was coming with his wife."

Fonda said they had been friends for years and the president has served as his pastor. He was quite comfortable with the President, but Mrs. Fonda wanted everything to be extra special because they were going to meet the President's new young wife.

I said I could be of help. I was first a houseboy and then the butler for a family. I could answer the door and assist during the visit. Mrs. Fonda overhead our conversation and said that I could be like a butler to the family at which Mr. Fonda threw up his hands and said if it would make Mrs. Fonda happy then so be it.

Although I wore the same shoes and pants, Mrs. Fonda found an old jacket and shirt for me. I put lard on my shoes which shined them up, but knew I had to avoid the dogs outside, for they would lick my shoes. I showed the maid how to fold the napkins to make them look sharp. I rearranged the table, just like I had done on the plantation. Also, to make it easier for guests to know which was the dessert fork, I placed it at the top of the plate. I removed the clutter of shoes and boots from the front hallway and put them into a small closet. The maid was so nervous.

Mr. Fonda noticed and said, "The Good Book says, Be anxious for nothing, but in everything by prayer and supplication, with thanksgiving, let your requests be made known unto God."

So I asked God for a good evening, calmed the maid down and told her I would serve the food if she had it hot and ready for plating.

Soon there was the noise of a carriage. I approached the front door, and opened it for the Fondas to greet their guests, the President Eliphalet and Mrs. Urania Nott. She was much younger than the president, but both seemed very happy as they stepped out of the carriage.

As they arrived, I took Dr. Nott's hat and coat and retrieved Mrs. Nott's coat from Mr. Fonda. They sat in the parlor for a few moments discussing the weather and moved right into the dining room for lunch. The maid handed me each dish—mashed potatoes, roasted chicken livers and onions, and cornbread with whole kernels throughout.

Now I realized I hadn't eaten all day and this food looked really good to me. After lunch, the men went into the study while the woman folk returned back to the parlor to talk. I went into the study and over heard the conversation.

Dr. Nott was asking Mr. Fonda how he could afford a butler. Fonda confessed and told him how anxious his wife was over having such respectable company and that I had come up with the idea. He told Nott it was all a "charade" which was a new word to me. He said that I was a field hand who was also good at handy work around the house.

Dr. Nott saw me in the doorway standing stiff – in the South most white folk don't even notice when colored folk are around and talk freely in front of them and about them as if they were invisible. Dr. Nott had noticed that I was there and was looking directly at me. I don't know why, but I felt like I was caught doing something wrong. But as I stood there while Dr. Nott was questioning Fonda about me, he looked at me with very caring eyes.

All I could do was shrug my shoulders. At which point he gave Fonda a "proposition"--this was another new word I'd have to learn. After listening to them, I realized that a proposition meant to make a deal. At this time, I had to leave them to help the maid in the kitchen. After they left, I helped the maid clean up and was called back into the study. Mr. Fonda asked me to take a seat on the fine leather chair next to his desk. He said that Dr. Nott wanted me to work for him. He said that Dr. Nott would pay me more than I was making right now. Dr. Nott said to him that I had good skills and seemed trustworthy and he needed a good man to work for him. He also said words that stuck with me:

"This is not a slave state, men up here in the North choose who they want to work for. I don't want to lose you, but Dr. Nott is my dear friend and I think you could be more of a help to him with him getting on in age. It is your choice if you stay here, I could only afford to pay you the wages you currently make. If you go, both Mrs. Fonda and I will miss you. But since Dr. Nott is my friend, I encourage you to consider helping my dear friend and pastor."

I knew I had a choice to go—a very different feeling than being forced to be sold away from family and friends. And with that, I made up my mind to go and work for Dr. Nott and leave my dear friend Washington and the Fonda family. When I told Washington what I was going to do, he confided in me. He said to me:

"You have been more caring to me than my own family. The Fondas have been just as kind with the promise of good hot meals, a wage and a home."

He said he missed the only family he's known, but he did not miss the heavy cloud they placed upon him for killing his mother.

I put my hand on his hand and looked him dead in his eyes and said, "It is a heavy undue guilt on your shoulders. You did not kill your mother. Your ma died giving birth to you. Many people are alive today whose mother died giving birth to them. It was cruel of your family to blame you for this. We are respected here in the North because we are good people and good workers. You will do well here, so lift that burden off your back, stand up straight and be proud that you are a good free negro man."

And with that, he stood up straight with tears streaming from his eyes, shook my hand and pulled me closer for hug. As he cried, his shoulder heaved, for all the weight had been lifted.

It was not until recently when I talked with Dr. Nott about my circumstance, that there was a clear distinction in my work as a field hand. On the Southern plantation, we worked in fear of the whip. We were not paid. We worked whether we wanted to or even could do and there was no respect for our work or us. On the Fonda's farm, there was a level of respect for our hard work. Our life with family and friends was acknowledged.

Our salary was a reward for a job well done – affecting our pride. This pride helped us to produce good work and many times we far surpassed the expectations of our bosses.

Chapter Fourteen

The Promise of a New City

Schenectady is a bustling city, famous for making brooms and at the edge of the city is Union College. There is a small but vibrant community of colored people and one big colored church for us to worship. A white man established the Duryee AME church for all of us colored people. Isaac Duryee had been a student at Union College and he saw a need for a church after hearing that we gathered in small groups in homes and halls without a church for many years. He also knew that those of us who did attend the white church sat separately in the back of the church. It was here at this church where I broke into a sweat and my heart skipped a beat for the first time.

It was in church where I fell in love. I feel God was with me when it happened. When I entered the colored church, I was still in the habit of sitting towards the back of a room, allowing the front for the elderly and large families like we did in the field house. I had heard about the church through Dr. Nott and, knowing he was a Christian man, I understood the importance of attending church.

He encouraged us to grow and feel our Holy Spirit and since I could not attend services on campus, which were only for students, faculty and their families, I decided to explore and try to feel the Spirit and find a church. I learned about our souls and damnation. On the plantation, we would worship in our slave quarters in the woods, but we didn't have one leader. The elders took turns teaching us about the Lord and praising with song and dance as the spirits moved us, 'cause we didn't know about all this talk about saving our souls.

I approached the steps of this church building, taking in the beautiful arched windows and brick bell tower. It looked like a beautiful smaller version of the college's chapel. Inside were people with many types of colored skin— light-skinned, dark-skinned. There were people with long hair, curly hair, no hair. I saw small, thin women in long skirts with white lace on their hair, older women with busy hats, men in suits and ties or white shirts and ties depending on age.

All were swaying and shouting "amens" and "hallelujahs" led by a group of women standing in front of three large chairs singing and clapping. I sat with two fellows a little younger than myself in the back. A rather large man wearing black with a white collar took the front chair facing everyone; I found out later it's called a "pulpit." He began to breathe heavily and talk of the Lord and Jesus as our Savior. I felt myself swaying with the men in my pew, they said "amen" and I began to get the rhythm of saying "amen" and "hallelujah."

The large man was the preacher or sometimes he is called the minister. He talked like he was singing a slow, long song but he was talking not singing. He wiped his brow with a cloth. As he ended each thought, we said "amen" in agreeing with what he said. He brought up interesting ways to please God and we said, "Hallelujah." The movement of the call of his verse and our response made me feel as if we were all in the house of the Lord together as one family. And I surely missed my family.

I started to go to this church every Sunday and one Sunday I noticed the most beautiful woman I'd ever seen besides my own ma. The church was hot and musty and the sun was shining through the arch window perfectly, sitting on the shoulder and small hat and hair of curls of this sweet-looking woman. On this day, she was concentrating on the women singing in front, mouthing their song, bowing her head in agreement and saying 'amen' to the message of the song.

She did not notice me; she was in a trance, with a slight smile on her face. I could only see her from the side and then my heart skipped a beat and I began to sweat. I thought I was ill, but one cannot feel this good and be ill at the same time.

They passed a basket around every Sunday for us to put money in for the church. Some put coins in, others dollars, but I noticed almost all families put something in the offertory. I got paid $10 a week and at first I only placed change in the basket. I noticed most men place a dollar so I began to put that much in the basket. Today is first Sunday, so we get to break bread together and to do this we walk around the pews to the front of the church. We take the host, a stale piece of bread, and a sip from the same bottle of sweet grape juice and return to our seats remembering the Lord.

I know this may sound like the Devil was in me, but I couldn't wait to take the host so that I might get a better view of this woman. As the church lined up, we went to the pulpit one aisle at a time starting from the back of this room and I was four pews from the back door. When it was our turn, I got up to walk and folded my hands in front of me and walked with my head down. I proceeded with confidence and then as I approached her aisle, I glimpsed to my right and saw her eyes meet mine. I was drawn into her dark brown eyes, the curls of her bangs hanging closely to her brow, and her smile. My knees felt almost weak and then I felt it, a nudge to my back as my pew buddy pushed me to move forward.

I realized the whole church was looking at me staring at her! I quickly walked up, took the host as the music swelled, there were more shouts of "amen," and I took another look to find her, but she was no longer in her pew. I put my head down as we made our way back to our seats.

As I sat, I prayed for many familiar things that day, Dr. Nott and his family, and two students who took ill last week. But most importantly, I prayed for my family back on the plantation, wishing they could feel the hot sun on their skin in comfort and breathe in a full breath of freedom. I also added to my prayers that I get to meet this lovely creature one more time before I die from heartache.

I looked up to the front of the room and the pastor was talking, though I didn't know what he was saying. I looked over for her, and she was back in her seat looking ahead and praising. And then I noticed it, she quickly glanced back and looked at me, dropped her head and straightened her back as she said, "hallelujah" a little too loud, but with meaning, and I was at peace and whispered, "Hallelujah."

As service came to a close, I decided I wanted to get outside quickly, partially due to the heat in church and partially because I wanted to be able to see her as she walked down the front steps. As I shook the Reverend's hand, he embraced it with both hands, placing his on top of mine and blessed me:

"I see the Spirit moved you to a standstill today."

I nodded in embarrassment and said nothing. He proceeded:

"You've been attending church for a while now. Good to see you and hope to see you at the church picnic on Saturday."

I had no intention of going to the picnic. I was not sure of my duties for the weekend at the college. He assured me:

"There are sure to be good food and good company at the picnic including folks who can stop you in your tracks," as he grinned and let go of my hands.

Now, I was ready to hightail it out of there, but out she came into the sunlight. Because she was on the steps, I viewed her from the ground up. She had on a simple black heeled shoe that showed a bit of her ankle under her black skirt, a sweater as blue as the sky, and curves in all the right places. When I went to look up at her fully, I couldn't see her face clearly as I was blinded by the sun, but I saw her hair flowing on her shoulders.

As she walked down the stairs, her hair bouncing on her shoulders, her face began to come into view. She had the cutest pug nose, full plump lips, and eyes you could get lost in. As she came towards me, a gentleman stood in front of me, hand extended, saying he was Deacon Johnson. He knew who I was, but hadn't met me officially and was glad to see me attending his church. That phrase caught me, 'his church.' Wasn't there a recent message that the church was the home of all people? He was talking about what he had done with the church and then he reached behind himself, very aware of his surroundings, and pulled forward the young lady I had my sights set on. A feeling of dread came over me for she could be his wife.

He said, "I'd like for you to meet my sister. Her name is Diana, but we lovingly call her Anna."

His sister! My mind came to attention as I reached out and received her small, delicate, gloved hand. She was looking up at me; she couldn't have been more than five feet tall, small and slender. As she said, 'hello' with a slight curtsy, I noticed a small quarter-sized mark on her right cheek.

She noticed me noticing her, pulled up her fan to her face and excused herself briskly. Deacon then said he would love for me to join his family table at the church picnic next week, and I agreed with some guilt. I must make sure to get the afternoon free.

Chapter Fifteen

The Future Mrs. Viney

It was easier than I thought it was going to be to get the afternoon free. These summer days without students on campus meant I only had to take the Notts to town for morning tea, do a bit of shopping and bring them back to the college. I had my own room in the back of the dormitory; it had a bed and a table with a basin. I took a bird bath, not a full tub bath that I remember enjoying on my first day of freedom, or even a dip in the river, but with cool water in a basin in my room to get the dust off.

I was eager to change into a clean shirt for the picnic. As I was leaving the house, I greased my hair with a little lard I took from the kitchen. I did not have anything to bring to the picnic until I remembered seeing boys in the field play games with balls so I asked the college sweeper for a couple of old balls and off I walked to the picnic cove.

A host of people were there, carrying baskets of chicken, ham, pig's feet, candied sweet potatoes, potato salad, pies, cakes and cookies. I heard somebody calling Moses and looked to see Deacon Johnson at a table with children running around it, two women setting out food, gentlemen gathered in a circle and then I saw her. She was bending over a picnic basket, pulling a multicolored quilt cloth out and placing it on the ground.

I reached my hand out to the Deacon who proceeded to introduce me to his four cousins, each greeting me with a tight handshake, his wife, with a curtsy, five children – ranging in age from 4-12 years and one in a tram—and his sister, Anna, again. She came forward, head a little bowed and to the side, as she gave me her hand with a slight curtsy. I took the little hand and placed mine on top and I looked up to see the deacon looking over her shoulder with a slight stern smile.

The adults sat around the picnic table while the children were on the quilt. The men talked of impending war and the threat to freedom, while the women talked about the children. I did not talk at all about my background, only to say my family was not from around here and I had a mother and father who raised us on a farm. After eating, we needed to unbutton the top of our pants, and some of the men laid back on the grassy ground with their hats over their eyes. The children went off to play, with the balls I brought, the deacon and his wife went for a walk and Anna and I sat at the table alone.

Neither one of us looked at each other as we sat in silence. Finally, she offered another biscuit and I asked what was in her biscuits that folks just kept raving about them.

She gave a broad smile and said, "Powder biscuits are not so easy to make—too much kneading and they become hard tacks, too much powder and they become bitter, too much milk makes them soggy."

She began to describe how she baked, and I stared at her plump lips, enthralled.

"I put in four pinches of powder, and you can only add enough milk to form a ball, to knead them perfectly." I smiled and said I was so full I could waddle and she suggested I should go for a walk. I stated, "Walking is much more interesting when you are able to share it with another. Would you join me?"

She quickly put dishes back in the basket and wiped her hands on her apron as she took it off. She grabbed her straw hat and purposely walked around the table to join me on my right for a brisk walk. We walked and talked far past the pond, watching ducks and geese and commenting on the number of frogs during this dusk hour.

Not noticing the time, we heard our names being called from a distance. By this time, her arm was locked through mine as we came back towards the cove and saw folks walking away. We caught up with the deacon and his family who were hitching up their horses for their longer ride home.

I so wanted to spend more time with Anna, and told her I wanted to walk her home. She said we needed to ask her brother. As I am learning the ways of these Northern people, I approached her brother.

"Sir, I'd like to walk with Anna to your home. We'd be there before the sun sets and I will always be respectful."

He brushed his hands on his pants and said with a serious tone, "Son, you know you betta be respecting her wishes or you will have to deal with me."

As I heard this, I was a bit shaken. I gave him my sweaty hand to shake and as I turned, I saw a bit of a sly smile on his face and I took a deep breath. I walked quickly over to the waiting Anna and we began to walk—with permission from her brother. I proceeded to walk her home, but realized I didn't know where she lived. She said it's a straight walk about four miles. She worked for the widow, Mrs. Bridges, as her cook and maid, and she needed to help her with supper.

We took our time walking, sometimes in silence, as she hummed a church tune and asked me to guess it. I asked a few questions about her life. When we reached the start of her street, she stopped. She looked up and asked me why I hadn't asked her about her mole. The word mole was new to me. I didn't understand what this meant. I did not quite know what she was talking about. She repeated herself:

"Why didn't you ask about the mole on my cheek?" I was honest and said, "I hadn't really noticed your cheeks--maybe once and I forgot all about it."

She said I forgot because she kept her face to the side of my sight so I could not see it, which explained why she always walked on my right.

She said, "I do not get many men calling on me because of my face; I'm ugly, and this mole will never go away. In fact, it could get bigger since it started out so small as a birthmark when I was a babe and is now the size of a lima bean."

I took her chin in my hand and tilted her head towards the light of the moon so I could see it better and, to my surprise, she let me. Then I looked back into her eyes, which were wet with tears and said, "It's shaped like the sun and is a beauty mark from the Lord. You should wear it knowing that it makes you unique. A ray of sunshine has fallen upon your cheek and makes you a real beauty."

Then I kissed her lips, so softly as I felt her hand take my arm and give me a squeeze. And I could feel my heart skip a beat again, and this time it felt good. She pulled back with a slight blush in her cheek, but I couldn't let her go, not yet.

My mind was craving for more, so I took her shoulders by my hands. She was short, but her shoulders were strong. I leaned her on my chest. We pulled slightly apart, she moistened her lips, tilted her head and closed her eyes, and I bowed to kiss her fully on her warm, supple, soft lips. She wrapped her arms around my waist and I realized she could hardly reach my shoulders, so I smiled while we smooched.

And she was mine. I didn't know at the time that it would have been more proper for me to ask her brother for her hand in marriage before I kissed her. I thank the Lord to this day that no one held my not knowing against me.

I began to attend this church every Sunday. I would assist Dr. Nott with his Sunday morning rituals, including a hearty breakfast, dressage and help out to the horse carriage. I'd take him to the front of the chapel.

It is a short distance and although the students thought we drove up to make an appearance, Mrs. Nott and I knew that the morning walk over was sometimes hard for Dr. Nott. I would then take the carriage out the college gate to Anna's church. By the time the sermon was over, Dr. Nott's joints would be loosened up enough for him to walk back to the house with Mrs. Nott.

This time when I entered the church hall, the music was lively with a strange-looking instrument being strummed, which they called a "geetar," and a man was also thumping on an unusual-looking drum. It reminded me of home on the plantation, not the tone, just the beat. I sat down and began to daydream about the sixth night of work when we were allowed to sit around a fire in the woods and play music. I could hear Pa say, "Boy, go an' fetch the banza," and I would run and grab the instrument, which was wrapped in a quilt on the floor in the corner. The banza was made of a gourd, shaped like a flat pumpkin and it was covered in animal skin.

I think it was deer skin and there were four strings that ran from its narrow neck to its base. Pa would strum the strings, which each carried its own sound. We did not have a drum on the plantation, but someone would find a pot or tin and bang the beat. Another would pick up the bones and start rattling a beat and we would dance and sing songs. These were real animal bones, some say they were brought over on the slave ship, others say they came from a dead bull.

I loved hearing it, the bones played, watching the finger-hand clicking of the sound. When played slowly, it sounded like horse hooves trotting; when played fast, the sound seemed to grab our bones and move us from within our souls. The stringed banza would start folks to sway and as the drum would step in, we'd start to clap. As the music got louder and stronger, the bones would cause our shoulders to pump up and down and some folks would begin to stand and clap and move their hips.

Then, we would begin singing, first starting out in a hum, then words from the leader would be repeated by everyone. Some of the words were not words that our white master knew, and some I did not know the meaning of. But the elders knew these words and we would repeat them in song.

One song that I remember and is sung a little different in the North was *Nobody Knows*. It goes,

Nobody knows de trouble I've had
Nobody knows but Jesus
Nobody knows de trouble I've had
glory, hallelu
One morning I was a-walking down
O yes, Lord
I saw some berries a-hanging down
O yes, Lord
I pick de berry and I suck de juice
O yes Lord
Just as sweet as the honey in de comb
O yes Lord
Sometimes I'm up and sometimes I'm down
O yes Lord
Sometimes I'm almost on de groun'
O yes Lord
What makes ole Satan hate me so
O yes Lord

Because he got me once and he let me go
O yes Lord
Nobody knows de trouble I've had
Nobody knows but Jesus
Nobody know de trouble I've had
glory hallelu

Some of the elders talked in a language I couldn't understand, repeating phrases they said they remembered from their ma and pa. This song caused them to wail and cry more than other songs.

Ma would say the spirits were all around, the souls of our people who had passed on, the memories of our free land of Africa and the stories that the elders would share. These spirits would come into our hearts and our minds as some folks sang and cried and others screamed and kissed and hugged the ground.

After a while, Ma, along with other women, would jump and spin around in circles until she was so tired she'd drop to the ground in exhaustion. One of the young'uns would run into her arms and she would hold him and weep this heart-tugging sob until she just gave up. Out of breath, she would sit on the ground until another song would come into her soul.

In this northern church we learned that to be absent from the body is to be present with the Lord. We all would be crying and praising, knowing that there was a better life. Elders who had many memories of this life and young'uns who dreamed of starting to really live it all held on to this glorious promise. We just had to wait until we passed on so that the Lord could take us there.

As a child I didn't understand much what these spirituals meant to my people. As I grew older and, more importantly, as I was planning my escape, these songs would sometimes enter my head and would keep my mind on my purpose. We must have known that a better life could be possible on this great Earth.

Our masters had a good life, and although we had a better life than other slaves, there must be a better life for us. Some say it comes with freedom and we did not have freedom. But we knew we had a good master, our whole family was together, we had no fear of being sold and had good quarters to live in. We were not chained and we were only beaten when the master was angry.

We ate the worst part of the animals—parts that the master's family wouldn't eat—but there was plenty of tasty food like pigs' feet, pig ears, chitterlings and hog mahs. We didn't eat the bacon or pork chops, but it sure was tasty. We also had chicken neck, feet and wings and cow tongue and tail, small pieces of bone and marrow for a good stew. And Ma would cook whatever greens she had grown in the garden and she'd make pan bread and turn our meal into a feast.

Pan bread was our favorite. Ma would mix flour and water until it was doughy and roll it out until flat. I loved to watch her cook. She would heat pig fat in the pan until it was poppin' and place the flattened dough in the hot grease. She'd flip it over, wait until the poppin' stopped and you heard sizzling and you knew it was ready. We would break off pieces, so hot to our fingers, and sometimes lick the salty grease off. You'd bite into the crunchy outside and taste the soft fluffy inside—hot and filling. Love me some pan bread.

I realized I was daydreaming in church and the music brought me back to my pew. I saw Anna once again, seated in the front rows of the church, and I smiled. I wanted her to be my woman. I knew nothing of the customs of the North and being free. If I were on my plantation, I would just need to say to my girl that we are one. There would be no talk of courtship, no gifts of jewels or a church wedding. On the plantation when we met a young woman who was interested in us and hoped she could bear many children, we would take her into our arms and kiss her.

We would be as a couple, and our family—or elders if we had no family— would be told of our wanting to be together. Many women slaves, and sometimes young girls on plantations, were at the will of the master or the master's sons. Many masters wanted women slaves to bed other male slaves, especially strong, colored slaves, so they could produce strong children.

This was an economic decision, to establish strong "property" for their master to sell. Mr. Murphy was a kind master, allowing men slaves to pick their wives and holding ceremonies in our own manner. By doing so, we were less likely to escape if we knew that Master Murphy was not going to sell us and we would not run away because we were allowed to stay together.

Our southern marriage ceremonies were sweet and meaningful. All slaves would meet in the forest clearing. Our spiritual leaders were the elder slaves who would share Bible verses they had learned. We would vow to remain together until we parted. This notion of "until we part" was said with sadness for we knew that at any time we could be sold away from each other.

To bind us together and start our own family, we placed a broom on the ground. We would hold hands as we faced each other. As we nodded, we would jump over the broom, trying not to separate. This moment was solemn for we would never truly be separated as long as we could hold hands, even for a moment. We knew that if anything happened to our master, we might not be able to stay together, not husband and wife, not child and mother, not brother and sister.

Tradition in the North was different. Anna said that we would be married in the church with family around. She said we could go to the courthouse for a license and this would make us legal. I was in fear of making us legal. What does this mean? Would my master find out about my wedding if it was legal? If my master found me, would Anna then become a slave? She could not survive a life on the plantation.

Anna also said that we needed time for courtship, at least one to two months so that we can get to know each other better. I had picked the woman I wanted to marry, but we still needed to wait until she was ready for a wedding. She also said I needed to ask her brother for her hand in marriage. Her father was dead and therefore I had to ask permission from the male head of the house.

I liked her brother so this was not difficult, but I did not understand why I needed to ask for permission. She was the one marrying me, too. Why couldn't she just ask him for permission? This seemed peculiar to me but I wanted to do right by this woman I loved. I also wanted her to know what was troubling me, but I couldn't tell her 'cause she might think I didn't want to marry her.

So I followed along. What else could I do? She said I had to court her for a while and so I did what she asked, which was to visit her and talk and go for walks. I loved her, so spending time with her was all that truly mattered. Although, as God is my witness, I couldn't wait to make her my one and only woman.

Chapter Sixteen

Making Wedding Plans

After the picnic, I visited Anna three times at her home on Hamilton Avenue. We would sit together in the parlor of her home. Although we sat on the same sofa with the respected space between us, it was clear that we should not touch one another.

It had been six weeks since the picnic. Every day I thought about her soft brown and black hair when it brushed my cheek. I would walk near the gardens on campus and the smell of the flowers would remind me of our short time at the picnic and I would ache to see her again. She told me all the courting ways I needed to do to greet her brother, so I vowed to give myself one more week and ask for her hand. Today was the day.

Her brother greeted me with a warm handshake. I took his hand in my right one to shake and placed my left hand on his upper arm, as we did on the plantation when greeting someone with respect. He seemed moved by this gesture and pulled me closer and shook harder. As we stood, I realized he was a very tall broad-shouldered man, which told me that I needed to get right to the point.

I began to speak, "Dear brother of the most beautiful woman I have ever met, I come to you today to ask your permission to wed your young sis, whom you treat as a daughter, Ms. Anna. I will treat her with much respect and will work hard to keep her happy and safe."

The brother, looking me straight in my eyes, started to say something. Then he suddenly dropped his head and took a mighty deep breath. As he began to look up he said, "When I saw you in the church staring at my Anna, I thought you were glaring at her with worry about her mole."

Seeing the confusion on my face he asked for forgiveness. "Oh, please excuse me. Anna did tell me that you call it a beauty mark. I agree. I've realized that her inner beauty, that she so lovingly naturally shows without words, caught you in surprise. At that time I knew she was going to be yours and that you would be a good man to her. You have my blessings."

I was so happy and nervous and so was he. We embraced, shoulder-to-shoulder, grip-to-grip and man-to-man.

But I had one more thing to ask of him. Anna had talked of a license to make it legal. I asked her brother to sit for I had a problem. I told him of how strong my love was for Anna and that I would never hurt her or leave her.

"So, as you see, my love for Anna is real in my heart, but I am not used to your ways here in the North. Now that we will be family, I must tell you my story. I come from a plantation in the South where I was a slave. I escaped to come north to the free states. I risked my life with two of my fellow men, but we made it and are enjoying our freedom."

He nodded and said, "Yes, there are many colored men here who still remember slavery, many of those who recently escaped tell us stories of their life in bondage. I was born in freedom, but I know my ancestors were slaves in the Carolinas. So please tell me what is your concern since you are free?"

As I tried to find the right words, I stuttered, "Oh--oh, well, Anna says we must get a license here in Schenectady. The license would make our marriage legal. I am afraid if we get a license then my master, who has power, would find out and come after me. I tell you, I will never willingly leave Anna, but I cannot get legal papers for fear that my master would find me and take me away from her. So as you can see, I do not know what to do."

Brother was not saying anything and I did not wish to look up into his eyes, so I kept my head humbly bowed. He began to speak. "Ah, my son, you need not get a license. God's law is higher than man's law. Man can only rightly confirm what God has established and God has never needed man's approval to do His will. And I believe it is His will that you and Anna be married. Our church has many members, escaped slaves, who are in fear of the paper bond of marriage that our laws offer. Many want to be married, but do not trust this law. Our pastor offers marriage in the eyes of God our Lord without the need for legal papers. Pastor said that for years the colored man and woman have always only been married under God's love and that is all that is needed for a wedding in his church."

I began to relax and realized that my eyes were watered. Although a tear did not drop, I cried within my heart for relief that I could marry my Anna without fear and with the full blessings of my new church family.

The Northern folks had unusual traditions. Anna was to wear a new dress, which she made herself with the help of her brother's wife. The dress was as blue as the sky, hugging her at the waist and flowing down to her ankles. When I saw her for the first time on our wedding day, I thought she was floating. Dr. Nott helped pay for a new jacket which would serve two purposes. I would wear it for my wedding and continue to use it on special occasions as I assisted him throughout my workday.

This jacket was new to me, having been given to me by his larger son who had outgrown it. Dr. Nott was generous to have a tailor fit it to my liking. My only memory of the wedding was the soft music and making sure to say, "I do 'til death us do part," and my Anna looking at me. We were surrounded by her family. For a moment, I had an ache in my heart that my people were not here. Sadly, my people did not know of the emotions that freedom can bring to the soul, did not know of the news of the world which comes so easily here in the North. Following our church wedding, Anna would join me at the college to work for Mrs. Nott.

Chapter Seventeen

My Life Working for the Notts

As Anna worked in South College cleaning and caring for Mrs. Nott's needs, I was working more closely with President Nott. He seemed very concerned about the state of the Union. I was closely watching Dr. Nott—his rheumatism was getting worse. There were evenings when he held onto my shoulder for security as we moved from the first floor dormitory in the library up the stairs to his bedroom where a stove fire was always roaring to help his joints keep warm and comfortable.

Mrs. Nott was so obliging and loving to her husband. I helped Dr. Nott while Mrs. Nott took the bed warmer out the fire and ran it through the linens so that he would be warm. Most times it was the housekeeper who was supposed to do it. I know that my Anna will be that dutiful to me as I age. Due to Mr. Nott's modesty about his wife seeing him in his true condition, I was starting to give him morning and evening massages to ease his pain.

Anna would heat peppermint oil, honey and a touch of beeswax over the fire until melted and smooth. I would rub and push the oils into Dr. Nott's skin and muscles. I'd start at the backside, rubbing in circular motions down the back of the thigh, behind the knee onto the calf and roll his ankles in my hands.

Dr. Nott would talk about his next speech, the message he wanted to send the young lads of the college—why they, as young men, were important to the world and that they must make a difference in the life of others. And as I would start his other leg, he would always bring these back around to moral and religious principles that should ground all decision-making.

Moses Viney in his long-time role as a cherished chaise driver in Schenectady. Union College Library Special Collections

When students misbehaved, he did not believe in heavy punishment. Instead he relied on "moral suasion," as he called it, to encourage better behavior. This also came across in his lectures and sermons. I would end the massage with a back and neck rub, rubbing out the stress of the day. The stress could have been due to a student's misbehavior or a gentleman's disturbing word on politics; they all take a toll on his body.

I rub in supportive words or agreement to the points that he's making, though there are times when I disagree and he listens patiently and ponders my words. When he is in a good mood, sometimes we get into a debate. The kind of debate we had allows one to hear both sides of an argument before making a final decision.

I will forever treasure his friendship because he always wants to make sure he knows both sides of an issue. I've seen this fairness when he entertains the opinions of Mrs. Nott. Not every husband allows such openness. Of course, not every woman has the strength of character like Mrs. Nott, and my Anna for that matter. Mrs. Nott is a most suitable helpmate for, Dr. Nott.

Mrs. Nott in Her Own Words

As wife of the president of a college, I am responsible for Dr. Nott and for all these boys on campus. These boys come from such good families, but many have gone astray from the values they were taught. Some come here because they could not control their youthful pranks at other institutions. Dr. Nott and I believe we need to give them a chance. As the students learn book knowledge and pay attention to their lectures, we provide moral solid ground. Some are rambunctious here as well, and others are the children of graduates. We must work closely with those youth, so they don't go astray.

There are times at the end of my day when I suffer from complete exhaustion. My work on committees to provide education to young women in the city is taxing. But I believe intelligent women raise intelligent families. When I come home, all of my time is devoted to Eliphalet. He is a very loving and caring husband and he is also headstrong. He is a good listener, a good man, a good husband and a good president. I love the passion he places on the campus community, ensuring that all students make it through college, by living in South Colonnade with the students. This living arrangement increases the likelihood of seeing that all students have good moral upbringing. I have a lot of patience for his headstrong stance, which is always for the betterment of others.

Since the arrival of Moses, my life has been blessed with ease of worry. We both are eager to make Eliphalet more comfortable and to meet his needs. There are times, without saying a word to each other, Moses and I will work together to ensure Eliphalet is cared for properly. Moses is strong and caring—two good qualities in the handling of this disease called rheumatism. You must be able to help move Eliphalet and massage, pulling and tugging the tight, tough muscles and inflamed joints. Moses shows patience while applying real pressure to the infected areas. He has been a blessing to both Dr. Nott and me.

At night, many times I lay awake not truly understanding how Eliphalet got the rheumatism. He is a good man, always putting others before himself. Why would the good Lord give him such a hard sickness? I know that we all have our own crosses to bear and I don't want to be ungrateful for the many blessings God has allowed in our lives. But it's still hard to watch those you love suffer through it all. Eliphalet is a man of faith and would never bemoan his condition.

If you asked him why he had the condition he'd reply, "Why not? God is using me. Is He not?"

My headstrong husband is so right. He works hard, lecturing and doing community work for these students, despite the physical challenges he faces every day. He does not move much in bed because lying stiff does not cause him discomfort. But if I join him and move just a little, I can hear a soft moan come from him.

It is a disease that produces pain so severe that Eliphalet is at times unable to stand and walk, moving stiffly and slowly to get around. Thankfully, Moses works on his body by moving and stretching his muscles with oils mixed with herbs.

I have the pleasure most evenings to do one special thing with my husband. There are times when we are talking about the day's experiences or when he's had some disturbing news and I can tell that he will not easily drift off to sleep. I heat a pan of water over the fire as if making tea. I place a jar of oil mixed with peppermint into the pan to get it warm. While he is lying down on the bed, I gently take off the many warm quilts near his feet. And as I sit down, I place a towel on my lap and lift his feet across my thighs.

I listen to him talk, giving him an "unh huhn" recognition every so often so he knows I'm listening. I dip my hand into the sweet-smelling oil, which has been warmed by the water. I rub his feet with my warm, oily hands, starting from the calf, to the ankle, and work my way down his heel.

He is usually talking about something that is disconcerting or that he's contemplating, but as soon as I start massaging, I hear a change in the rhythm of his voice. He slows down his pace of talking and sometimes I hear a small moan. I rub his heel and proceed to the inner part of his foot arch.

I press and pull at these tight points with my thumbs and fingers. I work my way up to the toes and take each, one at a time, and circle-pull them. I finish with rubbing from the back of his calves and front of his shins, to the top tips of his toes, replenishing my hands with oils so as not to rub dry his frail skin. I repeat this on the other hard-working, sweaty foot and by the time I'm done, he is talking slowly and groggy and drifting into sleep. This brings such pleasure to me, to ease the pain and take the strain of all the world issues from his shoulders.

I don't understand this disease. Parts of his body are not affected by the pain, which is in his bones and muscles. Most days his legs and hips are very inflamed, other days his hands, elbows and shoulders. He is such a strong man, but this frustrates him. By God's grace he does not see his disease as a weakness, continuing to send an image of strength to his students. When he goes into a sound, deep sleep with his chest breathing heavily, I slide his legs under the quilts.

I rub the oil on my hands, up to my elbows and arms. This feels smooth to my skin as I hug myself, put the basin on the table-stand, and sneak into bed. Next to me lays my strength, my world, my husband. It is my prayer that Anna becomes as much of a help as Moses has been.

Chapter Eighteen

Mrs. Nott and Mrs. Viney

I was worried that Mrs. Nott would not immediately take a liking to my new wife Anna. At that time, Mrs. Nott did not have a person whom she trusted in the household who worked for her. On one occasion, Mrs. Nott and I had noticed a shortage of place settings. One housemaid was let go when she was caught with two spoons in her apron.

The spoons fell out of her pocket as she tried to fold her apron over her arm upon leaving one evening. In another unfortunate instance, the cook, who had been there for many years was known to share a few stories with others on campus. These others included cooks who worked for students. Unfortunately, gossip from the house went out not only to other staff but sometimes to the students on campus.

Many of the past maids had been gossipers, sharing stories of the happenings in the house with the other maids in the city and also what goes on at the other houses on campus. As Mrs. Nott said, "If I want to make sure to get a secret out public, I inadvertently allow the maids to overhear my conversation. This will ensure that information gets out without my having to share it. I need a maid who is my confidante, someone who supports me and the work that the president and I do together. Surely folks know that the president makes all the decisions on campus, but he gets his ideas from others. He gets advice from our professors and students, but he also gets ideas and advice from me. I need a maid who, upon hearing these ideas, is able to remain quiet and not gossip about decisions we make before we are ready to share them. Do you think Mrs. Viney will be true in that manner?"

Although I knew in my heart that Anna could keep things very confidential, I truly did not know her well. I did know that she did not have many friends and seemed to keep to herself. So I said, "As you know, I have only known my wife for a little while. She is very reliable and responsible, as you have heard from the woman she worked for who does not wish to give her up easily but respects our marriage. I do know that if you make the point of confidentiality an important part of her job as housekeeper, she would be the type to keep every conversation private, and probably private from me, too."

Mrs. Nott smiled. I brought my wife to meet Mrs. Nott. My wife was dressed in an appropriate, beige cotton dimity, carrying her freshly ironed apron on one arm and her small basket on her other. I decided to dress well myself since I was making the introduction and wanted to make sure that Mrs. Nott saw us as a hard-working couple who together would be good help for her and President Nott. We were met at the back door by the cook and promptly seated in the kitchen. Although this is a Northern state, colored people must still be appropriate and enter from the back door.

We sat and I was nervous and sweaty. My wife, on the other hand, was sitting very straight, gloved hands in her lap on top of her folded apron. I questioned why the apron and Anna said assuredly, "If we are compatible I want to start right away today."

I smiled at the confidence of my bride and looked around the kitchen. This place was quiet now with only the cook remaining. The cook was taking inventory of what was needed from the market. In this kitchen there was a small table with four chairs in the center, a large fire place, an indoor sink and water. I was so used to going outside to pump water that when I first saw this I thought it was magic, much like the first time I saw a bathing room.

On the plantation we only had an outhouse. Even the master and his wife had to go outside to take care of business. The outhouse—some folks called it the backhouse—was a simple tin roof shack, and inside to sit on was a ply board with a hole in it. The hole was about a foot wide and about twenty feet deep although I'd never been able to see to the bottom of one. Every few years we filled the hole with dirt and moved the outhouse when the smell would waft across the field and into the main house.

There was a door with a moon crescent above it, indicating that it was an outhouse to take care of nature's business. At first glance, when I saw a commode and a sink next to it indoors, I thought it was "unsanitary," a new word I learned from Mrs. Nott, to have this inside the house. It is much more comfortable to relieve oneself outside, where the scents of relief are left for the wind to carry.

In the house, a bathing room is convenient, but there are times when the whole house might need a few extra candles to cover the sharp smells. Coming north, I learned about these differences. There were homes with pipes carrying water from outdoors to indoors and from indoors to outdoors to make the house more comfortable.

Mrs. Nott was particular to make sure we all did our jobs proper – most importantly the cook and the maid. As Mrs. Nott entered the kitchen, Anna and I both stood, me with my hat in hand, my wife taking a sweet curtsy. I introduced Anna, who nodded in my direction and made sure to take her seat after Mrs. Nott was comfortable. Mrs. Nott asked Anna questions and Anna answered with continued confidence. Then Mrs. Nott leaned towards Anna and, reading her body language, I think we both knew the difficult questions were about to begin.

"Who are your maid friends in Schenectady?"

"I don't have maid friends. I have two true friends, my brother, who raised me, and my pastor's wife. Oh, and now of course, Moses."

I smiled at this response with slight embarrassment.

"Why should someone trust you if they don't know you?" was the next question. Anna repeated the question slowly and replied:

"A person who doesn't know me shouldn't trust me. In order to trust someone or to respect someone you must earn that trust and that respect. This takes time, and it may take trials. Trials meaning that one must offer opportunity to show trust."

Mrs. Nott leaned back in her chair with a slight smile in the corner of her mouth. Then she leaned in and said, "I need someone to be more than just a maid, I need someone who will also be my confidante—someone who will work and plan with me and also hold all secrets of this household. You see, there are some who work here who share too many of the conversations they hear."

As Mrs. Nott said this, I saw the cook looking our way very curious. Anna straightened her back, looked directly at Mrs. Nott and said, "I live with my brother who is a deacon and my sister-in-law. Many times the pastor is at our house discussing the problems that are brought to him by our church members. They, along with their wives, meet to discuss some of these problems—parents with bad children, couples working on trusting each other, family sickness and death, all of which must be kept secret. Many times I am sitting in the room; they trust me not to share information. I serve them tea as they try to resolve some of the problems or as they find ways to handle a major issue.

"I understand being confidential with a story and also know how to be quiet and trusting. Although my sis-in-law and I sometimes do not see eye-to-eye, we are respectful of each other and both love my brother. After these conversations when the pastor takes his leave home, I see the weight of the issues on the shoulders of my brother, the deacon. Many times we, my brother, my sister-in-law and myself, will become comfortable on the couch and help my brother ease out of the pain that he is feeling for others. My sister-in-law rubs his hands, while I bring a cup of tea and a sweet for him to nibble on as he reflects on the meeting. I assure you, Mrs. Nott,

I am a very caring person who understands the importance of keeping a secret, of being a confidante."

Mrs. Nott looked at Anna with her eyes wide open and said, "You are a very remarkable young lady. You have insight and integrity, two good qualities to have at such a young age. If you are ready to start tomorrow morning, please be here by 7:00 so that you can go over with the cook and me your responsibilities. This way we can start the process of you earning trust."

I stood up and was about to take my leave, when Anna said, "Mrs. Nott, I would also like to get an early start with earning your trust. I brought my apron and would like to take this afternoon to get better acquainted with the household duties."

Mrs. Nott gave a soft smile, straightened her shoulders and said, "Well then, let me show you our home."

As they proceeded out into the foyer, I stood there dumbfounded. I caught the cook's eye. We both smiled and went about our day. The cook grabbed the shopping list and left out the back door, while I hung my coat and went out to greet Dr. Nott, having even greater admiration for my remarkable wife.

Chapter Nineteen

Understanding Anna's Story

I have no memory of my mother; she died a few weeks after the day of my birth. All I know about my mom is that her name was Gloria Diana, but everyone called her Diana. I don't know why, but she wanted me to be her namesake. She was a good church-going woman and she had a hard time carrying babies to birth.

My brother is 16 years older than me and there were a lot of miscarries of babies between the two of us. I don't know why, but I was told that Mom always had a weak heart. Brother told me that she would make a meal and become out of breath and tired. She slept a lot but I was told her mom, my grandma, helped Mom out until Mom died.

Grandma died when I was not even one year old. My brother tells me that my grandma was a freed slave, but he doesn't know the history. He did know that she was a mixed baby from the slave owners and that her mother's master set her free.

My father was a big man of a darker skin and worked hard as a blacksmith. Brother said, "Dad took Mom's death really badly, so bad that he couldn't call you Diana without tearing, so he called you Anna. He took to being at the blacksmithing shop which was hard work, but he made the best tools and people from all over the county would come to him for a good hammer, horse shoeing or sharpened knife. He died when you were almost three years old from an attack on his heart."

I only have one memory of my father coming in the door and I would run and hug this huge chest and arms and feel so safe. He smelled like hot burnt iron. To this day when I walk past the blacksmith, I always recall holding Dad's neck, smelling his hard-working body and feeling safe. I don't see his face, but I know it's him. My brother has a faded picture of Dad wearing his black apron with a big hammer in his hand.

At three years old, the only one left to take care of me was my newly-married, 19-year-old brother. They are the two people who I call family. My sis-in-law, who I call Sissy, says I was born with the mole on my face, which was left to me by my mom. She called Momma by her given name, Gloria Diana. Gloria Diana had a number of moles on her face and backside. Sissy and I never saw eye-to-eye.

I don't know what I ever did to her, but there were days when she was nice to me, usually when brother was around. There were days when Sissy would be mean to me, expecting me to do chores and making me watch my cousins, and getting mad when I didn't do something right. She wasn't vicious, but some days she'd be in a mood and would say things that were nice but also not so nice.

I remember when I was about 13 years old, one day after she came downstairs from one of her spells, she was in a strange mood. She walked slowly, dragging her feet. This was one of her spells that occurred after her headaches. She walked in the kitchen as I watched the youngest cousin while cooking supper and she said she had dreamt about my mother. She said:

"You need to remember that your mother Gloria Diana died with a heavy heart. Birthing was hard on her because she had suffered with a weak heart and bad blood for years. After your birth, when her heart finally gave out, God took her away from your brother who loved her so much. In my dreams, Sissy continued, Gloria Diana was crying 'cause she never got the chance to meet her grandbabies, my children."

"And you, Anna, never got a chance to love her like your brother did for she was so sick while you were only days old. But know that she loved and wanted you. You have been a burden to your brother, but he loves you so much. You owe your world to him."

She said this without any emotions and I couldn't tell if it was out of spite, but in her message she said something important. I have no memory of mother, but that was the first day I learned that my mom loved me.

My brother used to tell me stories about our mom, but they were always about what he remembers of her, not stories about her. He would say, "Mom knew how to read and write and was so beautiful. She was fairly brown like you, Anna, with long hair, but you have our father's quietness. He was a good man and tough on me to be good while Mom ran the house."

Brother never shared stories of what they did together, or whether Mom was a good cook. I would sometimes ask him to tell me a story about her and he would say "not now" or that he "didn't remember any stories." To hear from my brother's wife that my mom loved me, allowed me to forgive my sister-in-law for what I later realized when I got older was her jealousy about my relations with my brother. My first cousin was born when I turned four, so I was really the first child my brother had to raise and take care of. I owe my life to the caretaking of my brother. As for Sissy, as I got older, I knew that she had body and mind sickness that sometimes would get in the way of her tongue and cause her to say things I think she regretted or forgot after she said them.

My brother and I had little secret messages. We didn't learn to do this—it just happened over time. I think we developed these signals so as not to upset Sissy or to send a message to avoid her when she was in the bad mood. Sometimes, it was just a look with our eyes, other times it was a slight "tsk" sound that brother would make with his tongue. Our times together occurred when we met in secrecy—always outside of the home.

When I took the cousins out to the park, he would sometimes walk home from work or the church in that direction, clearly out of his way. He would play with his two young'uns, but walking back we'd put them in the pram with the new baby where they would fall asleep exhausted after play. He and I would walk and talk about our day before we got home.

Getting home, I would rush and get dinner on the table before Sissy came down from her room after a headache or stomach ache. She never did much around the house but eat and sleep as I watched the kids. The doctor said she was delicate and that we had to help her as much as we could so that she could rest.

As I got older, my body would get larger and so did the mole on my face. There are no pictures of me as a baby, but I remember the mole was so small that when I looked in a mirror, I could put my fingertip on it and cover it. I did not know the mole was ugly until I was in grammar school and the girls would talk about me out loud to each other. I was a little fairer skinned than they were and my hair was different, but I didn't mind their teasing on that.

But when they hurt me by calling me ugly because of the one big mole, not the smaller ones, I felt guilty because I blamed my mother. My best friend, Louise, was as fair skinned as I was. She would defend me and play with me. She never judged or teased me. She was also a lone child, raised by her grandma, who she called Nana, while her mother was a maid for a very wealthy family in Connecticut. Her father was said to have been a German, but although her Nana was upset for her daughter getting into the situation, her grandma loved Louise dearly. Nana was the first woman I ever watched give love to a child so easily. I also loved Louise 'cause she was as fair-skinned as I was and she was raised by someone other than her mother like I was.

As I got older I also worried about my womanly health. It was Louise and Nana who explained to me about my monthly. Sissy said my mother used to have painful monthlies and so did I. She said, "You are just like your mother, Gloria Diana, and you will probably never find a husband who could look past that mole. You will probably have difficulties bearing babies like she did."

She put fear in my soul, fear of the mole getting even bigger, fear that I would always be in pain once a month and fear that I would never be married and have babies of my own. But my brother always made me feel beautiful. "You will find someone who will love the beauty inside of you and all over you."

He would never have talked about me having babies, that was not man-talk. But he did say, "You should pray for and dream about the man you would want for a husband and the children you will have one day. This is the man I would want for you, one who sees the beauty within you."

As I got older, I just stopped thinking about boys. They had teased me so much as a child, pulling my hair and calling me Spot as if I was a dog.

My brother and I always attended church, always with his children and sometimes with Sissy, if she was feeling well. Brother would sometimes preach when the preacher was out of town. Brother's sermons were more dynamic than the preacher. Brother always had a good Bible story to go with his message.

But the true highlight of his sermon was the way he carried God's message to our church family. Brother always started out slow and steady, like the sounds of a carriage wheel, turning slowly rhythmically. And in his Bible story, he would always add something funny or interesting that we could all relate to.

As he would build up his sermon, he would signal to the organist who would begin to add low tones to emphasize each sentence's message. And the Spirit would move the church as women would swoon and cry out, "Hallelujah!" and the men would end each sentence with a hard "Amen." Then the Spirit would take over and the organist would play really fast as the guitar would strum and the drum would keep time. After a while, everyone would calm down, tired and weary. Brother's deep voice, which had sent everyone up on their feet, was now calming everyone down as he brought the story back to the beginning of his sermon to remind everyone what the message was as he'd get all God's people to say "Amen" in agreement.

Oh, those were the best sermons and it's a shame he only got to say those messages when pastor was away. Of course, the pastor's message was good, but, if truth be told, it just wasn't delivered as well as Brother's, at least in my mind's eye. Of course I'm partial to the brother who always gave me something to hope for and allowed me to marry a man of my dreams, my Moses.

Chapter Twenty

Saying Goodbye to Anna

The conversation with President Nott and the attorneys left me tired, worried and often on my knees in desperate prayer. Junior Master Murphy would not give a reasonable price for my freedom and Dr. Nott was very frustrated. After considering several alternatives: sending me out to other free states with money to last until I would find a job or sending me to Canada until the Junior Master Murphy accepted a reasonable offer.

They chose Canada. We thought that it would take about six months for an agreement to be made with the stubborn Junior Master Murphy. Dr. Nott knew a family I could work for and earn a slight income. He also stated that only I needed to go, not Anna, who could stay and continue her work at the house. He shared this information in front of the attorney and judge: "Moses, we cannot do with both you and your wife gone. Urania, Mrs. Nott, will need more assistance with you gone and Anna is strong. She has no children and is physically able to do some of the heavy work."

I took in all of this. I understood that Dr. Nott did not want to say that Anna would be needed to help him upstairs. I wished we had this conversation in private, not with the attorneys around, so that I could voice my concern. I am the man of my family and cannot be replaced by a woman.

I am strong. Running away to Canada feels cowardly. I need to build my family and want time with my new bride to prepare for babies, which will be impossible to do if we are separated. I wanted to say all of this, but instead I looked at my feet, nodded my head in understanding, which was taken as agreement, and left the room.

It was done. The decision was made and I had no choice. I knew this was the right decision, but would have wanted a say in the matter, but this was not to be.

That evening, I worried in our little cottage. Since our marriage, the cottage has become our home. It sits behind South College, built very swiftly by order of Dr. Nott as a wedding gift. For truthfully, there was no room for us in South College. Anna had made yellow curtains for it, which brighten the kitchen. I only noticed the curtains because on the day that she put them up, she delighted in telling me that they were my favorite color. I don't believe I had a favorite color, but she determined that yellow was my color.

She reminded me of this and said, "Remember the one dreary grey day as we walked the campus, I stopped in my tracks and gasped? I pointed to the flowers near the bushes and you thought I saw a snake and proceeded to shove me to the side and step between me and the bush. As you stood there to protect me, I began to giggle and pointed to the flowers. You stood more firmly and began to laugh out loud in almost hysterics, too."

We both began to laugh again at this memory. I tried to catch my breath and talk at the same time and I said, "I had never seen such a brilliant yellow flower. It looked like a Gabriel's trumpet—narrow at the neck and opening wide at the mouth."

As I had gazed at the yellow flowers along the edge of the dirt walkway, I realized that I never really noticed the flower. The beauty of the flower, later I learned it was a called a daffodil, had stopped Anna in her tracks. I plucked one, put it in her hands and held them tight with both my hands. I looked Anna in the eyes and I remember saying, "Yellow flowers were painted by the heavens and no matter where I go they will always remind me of you."

Anna attributed this to being my favorite color and I have agreed that yellow is my favorite; anything to keep her happy.

In the kitchen we have four chairs and a table for guests. We have one dresser and, for the first time in my life, we have one good-sized bed in our room. On the plantation, we had straw on a dirt floor where my mother sewed covers and would re-patch them with old rags. This was considerably better than other slave quarters where sleeping on a dirt floor with many other slaves was common. I was filled with pride when I first saw my new house given by the college, which Anna has turned into a home.

We also have an empty room, waiting for our future children to fill our home. Right now, we have a trunk in it that holds precious clothes my wife has made for herself. As I think on my home, our home, my daydream is caused to fade by the strong smell of onions frying in lard. Anna has made my favorite meal of neck bones, collard greens with onions, vinegar and hot sauce, and corn bread with whole kernels of corn through and through.

She knows that I need to leave her for a few months and she has been serving me such good meals that I plan on coming home sooner than that. To neglect my family would be shameful. I did not fight for my freedom to be a coward and leave her. But I know that for me to survive, I must go to a safe place until Dr. Nott buys my freedom. Today is Saturday and I will be leaving on Monday. These are two days I need to cherish. We eat in silence, both of us pushing our food around our plates. I know I must eat. The food smells so good. She worked so hard on the meal, but the ache in my heart is interfering with my appetite. I can easily eat the cornbread though. It's too good to leave on the plate.

She looks me in the eye, ah those lovely eyes, breathes deeply and places her hands across the table to reach out to mine. She mumbled, "I will miss you, you are my hunk of Heaven. And if you do not make it back, I will know you will be waiting for me there."

As tears build up in her eyes, I become angry, not at her but at the situation. I said, "President Nott and his friends have come up with the best plan. I need to be safe and stay free until I am truly free."

Anna replied, "I trust that Dr. Nott will buy your freedom and not sell you off. Dr. and Mrs. Nott are part of our family now and we cannot both leave them; there would be no one to take care of them. I know that this is best. I know you wish we had more to say in the decision, but Dr. Nott is a good man and knows the law. This is best?" She stares through me as she asks this question.

Though I didn't know of any alternative, I assured her that this was what was best. "Anna, you know Dr. Nott is a very smart and caring man. He and two very powerful men have thought this over. They are law men and have mulled over all options. We have prayed and God has confirmed that this is best." I said this firmly to convince her--and myself.

The next day, President Nott beckoned me into his library for a discussion. He asked me to sit down, which was not typical for I stood most when working. Dr. Nott stated,

"I know this decision was not with your thoughts. I want you to know completely why you must go north. If you were caught in Schenectady, there would be little that I could do to obtain your freedom."

"You could go out to Western New York near Syracuse where abolitionists are pulling together to fight the fugitive law. I heard Frederick Douglass was out that way. He even came to Troy, New York right here in our neck of the woods and was back in Western New York giving talks about slavery. They say that over a thousand people attend meetings when he talks. I also found out that he publishes a paper on slavery. Although this would be a good place for you, you will not be truly free. There are many slaves who head to Syracuse and continue to Canada to be safe."

I knew about Frederick Douglass and Anna and I were surprised that there was a colored man who was an escaped slave who was writing papers and educating folks about the slave life he had lived. Dr. Nott knew of Douglass and his work, but he felt Douglass was too well known to be kidnapped back into slavery. This was not the case for me. The Junior Master Murphy had nothing to lose by trying to come north to get me and everything to gain.

Frederick Douglass had escaped from the same county as I did, but he spoke better than most folks I know from the South. I learned how to talk better while working in my master's house—first from the younger Murphy and also when I was their butler. I tried to talk like the white folks and sometimes the other slaves didn't like when I did. Up here in the North, I tried to talk more like a Northerner, but they don't say some words in the right order and they speak too fast. So I just speak my own way, proper Southern words and not too slow so people up here understand. But the minute I'm around a Southerner, I lean into my words and feel right at home.

Dr. Nott was right. I don't know what I would do in Western New York. If I fled to escape slavery or live as an abolitionist, Anna would have to come with me. I'm not sure she was fitting to run through woods and live off the land, being a city girl. Dr. Nott said, "There is also talk of a war about to begin and we are not sure what would come of that. We want the Union to remain as one and slavery may separate the states."

Dr. Nott was also right that this temporary stay in a another country until freedom was bought is a better choice than always having to look over my shoulder in fear. Dr. Nott then asked me if I understood and if I wanted to go. I said, "I agree. There are only three choices: stay here and worry every day, take a chance and flee to the west with Anna but not truly be free, or leave for Canada for a few months until my true freedom is bought."

I sighed and said, "Of course Canada will be the right choice."

I felt relieved that Dr. Nott knew the importance of meeting with me to have this discussion—the final decision was mine. He has always been a man who looked at all sides of an issue. He wanted me to understand the choices. My respect for him is as strong as ever.

At supper on Sunday, Anna and I spent our last evening together. Anna had baked a pound cake with a full pound of butter. It smelled delicious, but it was difficult for me to take a bite. Anna came around the table and sat on the floor's oval rug we purchased together to keep us warm as she placed her head in my lap. She said, "Please eat, for I want you to remember my cooking and go North as a strong man knowing you will come back to me."

As I stroked her hair, I began to say, "As you say we must have faith. God is with us. This decision was done by wise men. I was there; I listened to all the possibilities. At first they wanted to prove the law was not real and could not be for the people of New York, but they picked up huge dusty law books, flitted through them—licking fingers to turn pages, and said with disappointment that the law is binding and that we had to obey the law.

"Then, they talked about hiding me here locally or even on the campus or sending me out West. But the law said

I was a fugitive so they would be in trouble for hiding a fugitive. This would not be good for Dr. Nott. So they wanted me to stay free and Canada would keep me free. I will be hiding for only a few months but I will be free and I will return so we can continue to build our family."

I felt better 'cause when she looked up at me she was teary but smiling. I smiled back, but realized I said this as much to convince her as myself. We went to bed locked in arms, as I covered her to protect her with my body, arms and legs. We woke up at midnight to sounds of crickets and joined them in celebration of being with their life love. And as the crickets sung, Anna and I passionately worked on having us being in the family way for my return.

Chapter Twenty-one

Arriving in Canada and Meeting the Palemonts

Upon reaching Canada, I was confused by the train station, a small building that did not have the grandeur of Schenectady. I rode the last car of the long train ride and no one questioned me. I had my ticket, wore my good jacket and showed confidence to anyone who looked at me. Arriving in a small train station meant it would be easy to meet the Palemont family. I searched the station for someone about President Nott's age, since he was a friend of Dr. Nott.

I was not sure if these Canadian people spoke English, but they did talk funny. It took a while for my ear to hear familiar words in others' conversations. Though they were speaking English, the words were not very clear. I stood waiting for someone to approach me, standing tall with my bags at my side near a wall. I didn't want to offend anyone so I just stood by the wall and waited. I noticed a man approaching another colored man, having a conversation and looking around.

He was a small, round, bald black man and he was looking directly at me. He came over, placed his hat in his hand and started talking. I was overwhelmed by his speech; he was a colored man, but he spoke like the other white people here. I concentrated on his mouth and realized he was pronouncing my name.

I was startled, as I dealt with mixed emotions. I was so glad he knew my name, but knew that communicating with him would not be easy. I'd have to pay close attention to these people when they talked. They did not speak English well—but to have the colored people speaking the same way would make this a long stay.

Slaves, when we spoke with each other, had our own language— more heavy-voiced with words that blended and moved to rhythmic motions. We cared about each and every word we said, getting to the point. We spoke to our elders with respect, didn't matter if they were or were not relations. The elders would tell stories of a life before slavery, how they ran free in forests as children, how they lived in large huts with all family members from children to grandparents, how they lived off the land, killing beasts and eating gourds of pumpkin and the meat of fish and cattle.

When we told our ancestors' stories we took time to describe the colors of our lands, our people, our music, our animals and our surroundings. The white man would say, "I went to the back farm, took the road yonder in the forest."

As slaves we would say, "I went to the back farm, through dark wet mud, sun was shining so mud would dry up on the road before too long. Soft, cold mud is best for walking in wit' bare feet and hearing the squish between our toes."

But when we were around white owners we only said: "Yes Sir," or "Yes Ma'am."

Usually we'd bow to show respect. And unless asked a question that required more explanation, that's all we said.

When I arrived in the free North, there was a difference in how colored people talked to white people. They were respectful and they seemed more equal but less equal. Most coloreds worked for a white person, but some worked for other coloreds. The man who shined shoes in the train station, he said, "Yes, Sir," and "No, Sir," but he would whistle and liked his work. He wasn't afraid of the men who he shined shoes for and he worked for himself. The blacksmith would take a white man's horse and would explain to the white man the reasons why the horse was walking with a limp. The white man actually listened to him. I could hardly believe it. The blacksmith was respected and he had knowledge that the white man didn't have. Imagine that—a black man, was shown respect for his knowledge.

Many of the coloreds in Schenectady worked outside of houses in the broom factory or on the railway. Some of the coloreds and the whites would get jobs for one or two days and would keep traveling west on the barges floating down the Erie Canal. What was surprising to me was that coloreds could go to school in the North. The school was on Jay Street in a room in the basement of a building.

They didn't go to the white schools, but they could go to school and were taught by a colored teacher. I was too old for school now, but was so glad my future children would be able to read and write and learn about the world.

When I first arrived in Schenectady and started working on the Fonda farm, if the opportunity arose for me to give an opinion, I would say brief statements. I feared the white man, but many times I was asked what I thought about the fields. We could talk directly to our white bosses, though we did this with respect. Our heads were bowed as we looked at our shoes. This was what I was taught. The colored man learned to do this for survival.

In Canada, this colored man did not have the sing-song way we talked in the States. He talked like some of the white men on the train. And as we were leaving, he said his goodbyes to the white train clerk, who waved back with a smile. I realized this is truly freedom when you can talk with the white man like a white man and not fear retribution but receive respect.

I also found out that Canada once had slaves! It was confusing to me that this big and cold nation had at one time slave masters and owners. Now they do not believe in owning another human and slavery has been abolished. They even had an Anti-slavery Society of Canada.

Riding to the farm, this man called Richard, whose last name I could not understand, talked until we reached a fork in the road. He pointed to his left and said something was out that way. I still didn't understand. He pointed to the right and said something about a "mont-real-all." I didn't know what or where that was, but I nodded and smiled and he smiled back.

He pointed forward and said something about a northern pole. That's all I could understand; maybe he put a pole on the road for people to find free country. I likened it to the North Star in the sky that I followed when we fled Maryland. He pointed in that direction, slapped his whip so lightly on the back of the horse, which, moving slowly, stepped forward in that direction, and I sat back on the wooden bench and felt my shoulders droop. I had been clenching my jaw and tightening my neck and I had a head throb. As the wagon moved forward to a steady rhythm, I relaxed a little, curved my spine and was pleased that we continued to use the Lord's messages of the sky to keep me free.

I had fallen into a slight dreamlike state and had no idea of time, when I felt the wagon lean to the left and right. Re-orienting myself, I realized we were off the main road and I saw ahead a large plantation with a huge white house smack in the center, two smaller houses on the right and I jerked so hard to attention that the horse whinnied with discomfort. I sat up straight and felt my stomach ache in fear, my legs wanting to run not knowing to where and my arms and shoulders tightened with anger.

Had I dozed off so deeply that I was tricked into returning to a plantation? Can't be—I knew there were some free people and slaves who were tricked back into slavery. I had never heard that the trickster could have been a colored man. This could not be happening, not to me, not this time. And what would happen to Anna? So many things ran through my head that I felt explosive, but I stayed stiff, sitting straight and waiting to see what was to happen.

Richard pulled the wagon to the front of the house. I had ne'er entered a front door of a house in my days on Earth. Before we came to a full stop, I asked him what was this place? He looked at me in wonder and he said, "The Palemont farm."

I looked at him, not realizing my bulging eyes and tight jaw was frightening until Richard took me firmly on my upper arm and said very slowly but still with a strange tongue, "This is not slavery, this is your new boss. Many coloreds who come here are afraid; be not afraid. We work on this farm. We get paid. We have families, and no one owns us. Do you understand?"

Though no words came out of my mouth and I was still a little mistrustful, I nodded. I was not able to open my mouth for fear I wouldn't be able to stifle a scream of anger at him. Although he said these things, I still did not trust him. I allowed him to help me off the wagon, but once my feet were firmly planted on the ground, I pulled away from his grip, took my hat off my head and nodded in understanding.

We both walked the horses to the barn, which was a big square building with a round roof. It was red and so beautiful I could not believe they put horses in it. Those horses were living better than us slaves had on the plantation.

It was very cold here in Canada where the wind blew through your clothes and into your bones. I could not understand what would grow on a farm like this. Richard talked about the need for more hands on the farm. I asked, "This Canada is so cold; what do you grow, cotton or tobacco?"

Richard raised one eyebrow up and cocked his head to the side—kind of reminded me of the dogs on my master's plantation. Then he said, "Oh well, we grow wheat, but the crop had wheat midge and was diseased. We now need more hands 'cause Mr. Palemont went and got more livestock."

I'm understanding him a little better and I asked what was "livestock," trying to understand his accent, which he said was some French and some English. He said with a slight smile, "Livestock are cattle and we need to get rid of the bad wheat and plant hay and oats. This will take all autumn and into the winter. So we need good men who can work hard and fast."

I looked onto the fields and there were men cutting away the wheat, but I squinted against the hard wind and bright sun 'cause I didn't think I was seeing right. There in the fields, which looked maybe four or six acres cleared, were men standing side by side clearing with sickles, but these were men who were colored and white. They were swinging and clearing and a loud bell was ringing as they slowed down their swing.

They began to walk toward the main house together. They were talking to each other, looking tired but laughing—colored and white. They walked over to a very short, round man at the back of the house. He was handing them all money. Every one of them got money! They were slapping each other on their backsides and walking away. I'd never seen coloreds and whites having a good time together. Now I definitely knew I was in the land of the free, freer than New York.

As Richard and I came closer and the field hands were walking away, I asked him, "Where were they going?"

He said to their homes. I pondered this for a minute and looked around for a log house or cabin, but they walked down the road we had come in on and kept walking. Richard seemed to sense something was wrong.

"You will live here with us, but the field hands go home at the evening bell to their families. Some live close by and most live two to three miles down the road. Every day is payday and so some who don't know how to save for another day will head to town for a good drink before calling it a day."

Mr. Palemont, I assumed, closed up the box that had the money and looked at me with a big smile. He reached out his hand—yes, reached out his hand! He shook mine and said, "Welcome to Canada," but with a very soft voice where I would hear his French, 'cause the folks here come from across the seas just like my ancestors. I think the reason he didn't mind touching a colored man, the reason why he lets white men and colored men work together without a field master standing over them yelling orders, the reason why he reaches out to shake my hand, is that we have something in common. We both have ancestors who came across the great seas, so they must have been strong, honest and hard-working people.

He gestured for us to go in the house—through the front door. Yesiree, not the back door where I was heading until I noticed Mr. Palemont was still talking to me and walking or leading me round the front of the house. We entered the front and scraped the mud off our shoes. He took off his work shoes at the door and slipped into black low shoes. Richard backed out, tipped his hat and said, "See you in the morn."

Mr. Palemont gestured for me to take off my shoes. I'm not sure why, but I did it, with wonder when I will put them back on. He pointed to another pair of low, soft shoes and I put them on as I quickly followed him into the house. As we walked he said, "Those slippers are yours so not to track mud into the house. We do not wear work or street shoes in the house or Bessie will whip us with her broom."

There is so much space here, walls that seem to push up the roof with arches.

I remember how I was first struck by the dormitories of the college where I lived with President Nott. The walls and floors are far from the ceiling and the windows go from the floor almost to the roof. Here I saw two stuffed sofas which seat about four people, one large chair and one "pee-an-no," which I recognized and was proud I knew its name. He sat in a chair and a woman came in with two large dark metal mugs and white clouds floating on top.

He took one and I took the other, but I'm not sure what this is. He put the metal to his lips and as the white clouds floated down the side of the cup, he guzzled it down, licked the top of his lips, and smiled. I do the same, though I know not what I'm doing. The drink is warm, the clouds are smooth on my lips, and I feel my throat burn but welcome the drink.

Mr. Palemont talked of the hard work he has to do to get rid of the wheat disease. He was talking soft and fast. I was not understanding him and the warm drink was running inside me. He told me I would be sleeping in the backroom with the housemaid and butler. The maid, whose name was Bessie, was colored. The butler was what we called on the plantation a yellow man with slanty eyes.

I found out later that we should not say this 'cause they don't like it. Bessie says they be called "Chi-a-neese" so as not to insult them. Mr. Palemont finished his drink and told me I would get in pay what all of field hands make. Even though Dr. Nott was his friend, he couldn't pay me more. I said, "I was much obliged for the job and would work hard with the others."

The yellow man, whose name was Lok, said nothing, nodded for me to go with him. So, not to be rude, I drank the contents within the rest of the mug, stood up with a sway and shook Palemont's hand. I followed the "Chi-a-neese" man through long halls until a door opened with a short bed. I don't remember much more that night, but woke up with warm blankets on and my pants off.

My first morn here in Canada and my head was heavy and hurtin'. As I got out of my bed, I noticed someone had put on a fire and there was water in the washbasin. I wondered who was taking care of me? I felt the water in my hands and put it on my face, feeling my morning whiskers. I realized I was the one that did this for President Nott and as I awakened, I wondered who was doing this for him now. And my stomach hurt as I realized I was thinking about my Anna and missing her so.

I found my pants on a chair and pulled them up. The sun was beginning to show through the grey clouds and I wanted to get outside to work. I slowly made my way to the stairs, but looking down the three small steps caused the front of my head to hurt. I made it to the landing, holding on the banister. The sweet smell of molasses was pleasing to my nose as my mouth watered. I heard Bessie beckoning me to come into a room I had not been in. I pushed the white doors open and saw her standing in front of a black iron oven, and there was a table in the center with chairs around. She was talking and as I entered through the door it swings out, and in, and hits me in my backside.

This startled me. Bessie gave out a loud hooting belly laugh, which caused me to laugh along with her. To my surprise Lok was grinning as he was sitting at the table. This was the first time I had laughed in a long time. Bessie had a low deep voice and said, "Rest your feet. The hotcakes are almost ready. The other hands will be here soon and you need your food to work a good day. Your day will start with a morning meal; then you go off to the fields. When you hear the bell, supper will be ready and you come in. Lok will bring you water or tea in the midday, depending on how cold or hot it is outside. It is cool today so you might want to wear your nightshirt under your dayshirt. Now don't waste any time—eat while it's hot; then get to work."

The work day was hard, but the workers all gave their best. I got to thinking, the work day goes by faster and easier when you are not threatened with the whip. The midday supper was not what I was used to, potato in my soup was new to my tongue, and the fresh bread was hard on the outside and hard on the inside. The fellows said to dunk it in the bowl to eat it.

Although it was sloppy, it was good and filling. The rest of the day went fast and as we walked away, I realized I was looking forward to the next day even though I was still missing my bride.

Chapter Twenty-two

Anna and the Midwife

Moses has gone and left me as his new wife, with few chances to be blessed with a baby. Moses and I had talked about having three to four children—not too many that we couldn't afford them and not too little that we would worry about loss. We had been wanting to save a little money from our wages from Union College to have a family.

We started to work really hard on making babies. He had been gone only a few weeks when one day I needed to see a woman's doctor to find out what was wrong with me. I was now suffering with cramps and unmentionables every day. Since this was women's work, I talked to Sissy who gave me the name of the midwife. I needed to get over to Hamilton Street on the hill, where the midwife who worked with colored families lived.

I took in the breath of free, brisk air with deep satisfaction. My husband will be leaving for a few months and will come back a free man and hopefully a father. I don't know how he will feel about freedom, but it must be like breathing in for the first time without fear.

I have never experienced being owned by someone. I have felt obligated to my brother and family for watching over me, but never felt like my freedom was taken from me. Although I am cramping on my walk to the midwife, I am also wondering if my cramps are only due to the stress of the worry of my hard-working and gentle man. As I turned the corner onto Hamilton, the houses looked well-kept. The whole line of houses had colored people on their porches, some working in their gardens.

I asked for the midwife and they pointed to a small-sized, brown brick house with black trim. The house was pleasant, with hanging flowers on the front porch flowing in the wind, which also slightly moved the rocking chairs on the porch. I dreamed of rocking my baby to sleep. I tapped on the screen door.

Greeting me was a large woman of about 40 years old, with one child on her hip and an old, brown spotted dog softly barking at her feet. She stood and grinned a big, toothy grin and said, “Please ’cuse Max. He’s blind in one eye and can’t see out the other. He’s old, but does his best to try to protect me. How can I help you, Ma’am?”

I asked her if she is the midwife. She nodded and opened the screen door.

“I am the midwife called Miss Johnson, brought over 80 babies into this world, this here little one being one. Her mom is cleaning a home in the Stockade and will be here shortly. Let me put her down.”

As she took care of the baby, I took off my coat and gloves and looked around. This was the cleanest kitchen I’d ever seen, everything in its proper place. You could eat off the floor. I must ask her how she cleans her floor.

"So now, tell me what you need. I see you're a Mrs., with that nice looking ring. Either you are about to have a baby, and Ma'am your waist is too slender for that, or you want to have a baby."

Well, I must say she is a clever one.

"Miss Johnson, my name is Mrs. Viney, ah, Anna. I want to have a baby, many babies. We've been married awhile now and no babies. Now, I am cramping so much and every day I get my monthly with heaviness. I am tired all the time, but I am a good worker so as not to lose money. I clean for the President and Mrs. Notts over at the college. I want to know, is there something wrong with me?"

I asked this, but I was not doing a great job holding back tears. Miss Johnson looked at me and took my chin in her hands.

"Ma'am, there's some of us who can have children but no means to take care of them and there's some who have no children and want them more than honey. I'm not sure what ails you, but we need to examine you and figure out the problem. Why don't we go in my backroom and give you an examination to help you put your mind at ease."

She led me towards the back of the house and opened a door to a bright clean room with no windows.

Now I heard of white washing a fence, but it looked like she whitewashed this entire room. This room was cleaner and whiter than the kitchen. All that was in the space was a wooden table in the middle of the room with drawers under it. I had never seen such a table. She asked me to lie on the wood table and as I did, she pulled out the drawers and stuck the heel of my shoes in the ruts on the drawers. As she examined, she talked on and on about the little baby crawling and trying to walk, but I was not paying attention.

I had never been to a doctor, and no one had ever looked up my petticoats. I didn't know what to do or say, but if this was the way she would fix me and get me to have babies, I was willing to lie here. When she was done, what I experienced was uncomfortable but did not hurt. With her back to me, she asked me to get dressed and sit on the table. Although my back was hurting after her examination, I did feel relieved.

"Mrs. Viney, Anna," she said with more seriousness, "you may need to take in more food that gives you energy because you are having your womanly ways every day and this is too much and makes you weak. You need to be strong to get a baby and carry a baby for months. You must eat more meat and liver to get your blood stronger. You must rest at least once a day for about 20 minutes until you get your strength back. This should be in about 10-20 days."

I looked at her feeling hope that we will soon have a family and I dreamed of Moses bouncing a fat-thighed baby on his lap as I felt full of a second wonder in my belly. I realized I was not listening to her as she said she wanted to see me back in one month to see if I needed another exam. I didn't know why, but I felt the need to get to the butcher and pick up a slab of liver or a roast for supper.

"Thank you, Miss Johnson. I will see you in a month and will surely eat more meat."

As I left her home into what is now a mild, drizzling spring shower, Miss Johnson says, "Now don't forget, if you get worse you make a beeline over here. You may be able to have a baby, but we have to wait and see."

I wanted to stop and go back to ask her why she said I may be able to have a baby, but the rain shower was getting stronger and I was too elated and wanted to get to the butcher, so I put that notion out of my mind. I must get stronger in order to have a baby and meat makes your blood strong. I wish my Moses were here.

Moses Viney in his later years, still plying his daily trade as a sought-after chaise driver. Union College Library Special Collections

Chapter Twenty-three

The News to and from Canada

Months passed before we heard from Dr. Nott. He sent a letter to Mr. Palemont, who read it aloud to me, Bessie and Lok. We three have been spending evening times together sharing stories and learning about each other. He read the letter:

"My dear friend, I am pleased to hear of the safe arrival of Moses Viney. My son is in Maryland and proceeding with negotiations with his former master. My frustration with a man who calls himself a master and a Christian but does not understand human decency has taken a toll on my health.

Mrs. Nott tells me I have to remain calm because the state of the Union is going to have rough times ahead. We might be going into war if we don't resolve this slave issue in the States. Canada has more reasonably-minded politicians though our separation from England was indeed a necessary mark on history. I will post a letter as soon as I hear more details. Give my regards to Moses. His wife misses him but is doing well and his welcoming nature is needed back here at the college.

In the bonds of friendship, Eliphalet Nott."

As Mr. Palemont read the letter my heart was heavy with gladness to hear the good news of negotiations in

Maryland mixed with sadness of missing my Anna. I am not allowed to contact the college so I will wait for the next letter to arrive and will work hard for Mr. Palemont in the hopes that my good work will lead to a good deal in Maryland.

Anna's Thoughts and Fears

These days are so busy at the Notts and with the college, which is welcome as every eve is long 'cause I have too much time to miss my Moses. I spend my mornings up before the dawn, watching the sunrise, knowing this is a day closer to him coming home. I drop down to my knees and say my morning and evening prayers for his safe, free return.

I wear his shirt to bed so I can smell his body and feel his presence next to mine. I mourn to take it off as I need to wash and dress and head over to South College from our cottage. I smell the hot, greasy bacon from the kitchen as the cook has to make breakfast for the Notts and all the boys who live in this dormitory. With Moses not here, I help Dr. Nott from bed to his washbasin, but do not stay in his room for modesty's sake. I help Mrs. Nott, who is always dressed properly, with her hair neatly groomed.

I help her to lock her dress buttons. She is a stylish dresser, today wearing a white and blue dress, with a bow tucked neatly under her neck. Her sleeves are a bit sheer, with ruffled sleeves to show off her delicate, small hands. Though Dr. Nott moves slower than the Mrs., he always seems ready to meet her for the walk to the dining hall, though I am always at the ready to button his shoes before they go.

While they are gone, I tidy up the bedrooms and prepare for the day's schedule of a luncheon, a tea and several meetings for both. Mrs. Nott attends some of Dr. Notts' meetings and though she doesn't say much, she is a good listener. She holds meetings usually with other women about the necessity to provide good education to young girls. I'm thinking I would prefer if they first start with improving the education of colored boys who grow up to take care of families before educating white girls who grow up to marry white boys who have an education. But I can't say anything; I just think about these things sometimes.

After all of the guests leave, the Notts always go into the sitting room for a cup of tea. This is their quiet time to discuss whatever problems have come to light—usually about prohibition, slavery or the impending war. The other concerns they have that require complete privacy is when they discuss their finances, the college's finances, and work on getting money for the college so that these young boys get a fine education and the professors stay committed to teaching.

They like to keep these conversations to themselves and only let me, or Moses when he's home, in the room during this time. I feel at home in their rooms in the dormitory and stay all day until supper is served. At the end of the day, Mrs. Nott helps me get Dr. Nott to the bedroom where I have his night gown laid out for him. I also make sure that his clothes are laid out for the next day. Normally he wears the same outer clothes, but he likes to wear clean under garments every few days or so.

Some nights, I brush Mrs. Nott's hair and tie it up. Some nights, Dr. Nott asks me to bake something special for a guest arriving the next day. So I like staying up to gather flour, sugar and other needs and set them aside for the morn. My biscuits and dinette cake are so delightful that even the cook becomes eager for me to bake a treat so that she can taste a morsel.

I like the cook; she has a belly as big as her heart and is as round as she is tall. Her name is Winefred and she has long dark hair which comes down her back in a braid. She says she is Italian and she speaks with an accent from a country called Italy. She likes to cook different types of spaghetti pasta; They are all different shapes and sizes, but they all taste the same to me.

What makes each meal different is what she does with the shape of the dough. The shape I like is when she makes two small almost round shapes, puts meat in the middle of one of them and covers it with the other, then squeezes the sides and boils them. The Notts like when she rolls out the same dough and slices thin ribbons with a knife. All of these shapes are cooked the same, either they will go into hot boiling water until cooked, or cooked in tomatoes, or in the coal oven until they bubble over with heat through and through.

When the boiled pasta is cooked, she pours either a white or a red sauce on top. When she is in a good mood she makes a brown sauce. The brown sauce takes all day to cook and usually has pork and beef in it. All of her recipes have cheese either in it or on top of it. It doesn't matter what she cooks; there is always cheese and the boys love to eat it. For myself, I get tired of it sometimes.

On the Sunday when the cook has off, I make meals for the Notts and another one of the maids makes meals for the students. Since we all have to be at church, only two meals are made for the day. It doesn't matter what I cook; Dr. Nott only wants to know that the biscuits are baked. He smothers them with butter, while Mrs. Nott prefers apple butter or blackberry jam.

The most deep, darkest times are the nights; they feel long and heavy and empty. I arrive home, hopefully exhausted so that I will drop off to a hard sleep. Most times, I sit at the table thinking about my Moses.

Every night, I peer out the window to find the North Star. What is lovely to know is that when I look up at the star, it places me closer to Moses up north. This star has so much meaning to us. The North Star was Moses' guide to find his way out of the tunnel of slavery. I wonder as he followed the star, would he ever have thought that he would have to continue the journey after he had already found freedom?

I picture him working on a farm in Canada. I don't think I've ever been to an actual farm, living in the city. My brother always went to a farm to get the best meat, especially turkey or lamb. He loves to eat and I love to cook, and this works, since Sissy doesn't cook at all. I prefer baking over cooking though, and my peach cobbler causes everyone's mouths to water. Lord, forgive me for being vain.

My time with the midwife is not as productive as I would like. I am still not carrying a baby. I am taking some medicine and bitter tea as a remedy to the cramps.

I'm frustrated 'cause we know that we can't determine if I can have a baby with Moses away. Lord, I need him to be home so we can try to have a baby. Now, as I stare up at the star when I can find it in the late, dark skies, I find comfort knowing that he is looking at the same star and thinking about me. In the tension of the states and with the worry of the college finances, the vision of the star brings a peaceful comfort. These thoughts help me relax enough to fall asleep as the morning comes quickly and the work begins again—another day without him.

In the Mind of Mrs. Nott

Everyday Eliphalet and I meet and greet our politicians, friends, students and faculty. As the President's wife, I play no part in the discussions of the grown men, considering they would not take light of my opinion—publicly. But when Eliphalet has one of the young students in for a lecture, usually about their poor judgment, I chime in to make sure a motherly voice is heard before they depart.

Our evening discussions focus more on the impending war, which would happen if the North doesn't make more agreements with the South about slavery. The North wants slavery abolished. The South is so stubborn about their narrow view of slavery and preaches about how ending slavery would affect their livelihood. I think that it's fine for a colored to work on a plantation, but he should be paid some wages so he can support a decent Christian family.

You cannot keep them enslaved and sell off their wives and children. And if the women need to work, so be it. There are many a household up here in the North that could use a good colored woman and we will pay them a proper wage.

Well, I must say, I didn't expect Eliphalet to miss Moses as much as he does. My poor Eliphalet, I think it's the evening light that makes him melancholy over the fate of Moses. He stiffens up the most in the morn and in the eve and that's when Moses was most obliging to his needs.

It's also when Eliphalet lets out his daily frustrations, usually about prohibition laws needing to be shared with the people of our nation. But more recently his frustrations are steered by the ongoing conversations, both public and private, about ending slavery. He said to me once:

"Slavery should have ended with the British. Now, with our boy down in the South being a man, trying to buy Moses' freedom, we are both worried. These Southerners are not wrapped up too tight in their heads and get notions of people taking their property—colored folks. It makes me sick to my stomach. I pray our grandson keeps his wits about him, makes the deal and comes back high-tailing for home."

In the meantime, I will continue to soothe Eliphalet's anxious moments. He always seems to calm down with a soft foot rub as he turns to the quietude of a deep sleep.

As for me, I am getting a little worried about his aging years. I know I am 30 years his junior and he has outlived two wives, but I think his health is deteriorating, so I must begin to plan for my future. Though the thought of this causes my heart to sink deep into my womb for he is the man of my soul, who God has brought to me.

Anna seems to be stronger without Moses. When she first started working here, she was slumped-shouldered and bowing. Now, she stands tall meeting our eyes, making decisions on her own and being very polite. I think she is proud of the work she does for the college.

As always, her uniform is always clean and neat, and she is always punctual. Since Moses has been gone, she arrives earlier, works hard all day, doing work for both Dr. Nott and me. I don't know if I could be as strong as her with my husband in a different country for several months, and it looks like his stay may take more time than we estimated.

She seems to be considering her situation. She is taking time off to see the midwife. When Anna now talks of the days when Moses returns and her plans for their future she seems more confident. I am not sure what my future will be, but I have put much time into the future of other young women. The schools I've established in Nassau and Troy for the betterment of women have been very successful.

Now I must begin to plan for my elder age, and I know that Eliphalet may not be around to share this time with me. I don't cherish thoughts of being without my soul mate for a long period of time.

Chapter Twenty-four

Dr. Nott Worries about the Civil War

It's been well over one full year since I've seen my Anna. I've learned a lot about the people of Canada and their ways. Mr. Palemont speaks English and French and he is very liked by almost everyone in town. He treats all his workers with respect whether they be colored, Chinese or white. After our many gatherings with Lok, I also learned that they are called Chinese, not Chianeese. We get good pay for good work. The winters are hard on my skin, which becomes grey and dry. Bessie gives me lard to rub on my skin every morn before I go out in the bitter cold. My lips were hard and would split open and bleed, but a little lard on them made them smooth and feel cool.

My job today is to cut wood for the winter fires and stack it up. I love this job! There's a big pile of wood that I cut up into smaller wood and stack until there is a big pile of wood. This work leaves you with satisfaction because the work has a beginning and an end in a few hours as opposed to farming that has lots of time between planting and harvest. And I love the pleasure of knowing that this work will keep us warm for the winter.

As I do this work in the daylight, I see what these people call Canadian geese. I don't know how they know that the birds are from Canada; they could be from any nation flying here. What I do know is that they say the geese leave us in the winter to travel to warmer country. They return in the spring when we begin to prepare the ground for seeding. I saw this happen early last winter but was sad to see them come back in the spring because I had hoped to be back with my Anna by then. Here we are in another winter season in the most coldest place working so very hard and I must go to bed each night alone thinking about Anna alone as well.

Tonight I could not sleep. When I can't sleep I go into the parlor and look out the window to find the North Star. This is the star that led me to freedom and now it gives me hope for my soul to connect with Anna's soul. Just as I start to fall asleep in the chair, I feel a presence behind me in this dark parlor which only has the sliver of light from the moon. I look around and there is Bessie who has wandered in and is sitting on the couch.

She slightly giggles and says, "You miss ya woman and want to be with her."

I tell her yes and that we did not have much time together between the marriage and my coming to Canada. She says, "I don't know what it's like to be a slave. I was born here and gonna die here. What I know is that the man I love comes home for a little while and leaves every year for a long time, sometimes months, sometimes years.

"When he comes home we relive our love like newlyweds, which is why we only have two children, eight years apart. When they got older, I sent them to the city to live with my sister so they could get a good education. My husband is a proud man; he hunts all over the provinces bringing back furs. They are then turned into stoles or hats or coats of fox, seal and bear; people who can pay for them wear them for warmth. Your wife knows you are safe here. I worry every day for so many things can happen to my man. He could get eaten by a bear. He could fall through ice and drown. He could get frost bite, lose a leg, or freeze to his death. He is a good man, a hard-working man, and I pray every day that he comes home unharmed."

As she continues, I notice that she is sitting with her hands folded as if giving me a lecture like the professors at the college. She says, "You live in this house, work on a plantation and very little harm can come to you. Your wife is blessed to know that you are safe here and you do not put yourself at harm every day. Your wife knows that when you go back, you will be like newlyweds and have babies of your own and you will never leave her again.

"I know only that one day he will come home alive, injured or dead. If he is alive, he will stay until he is fattened up again, until he gets his full of me and my cookin', and until he has the energy to go back out hunting. Sometimes it's months, sometimes it's years and one day he just might not ever come back home."

I look at her and her eyes are filled with tears as they run down her cheeks and she does not wipe them away. She is not embarrassed by sharing her story and not angry at me and my selfishness for thinking I was not blessed. She is telling me her story and I feel her hurt.

She wipes her tears with the back of her wrist and gets up a little more slowly than she moves otherwise. As she walks towards me, I stand very still. She looks me in the eyes and places her large warm arms around me and her head on my shoulders and I feel her heaving and shaking. I wrap my arms around her and begin to allow my watering eyes to drop a tear that I feel roll down my cheek. I catch the tear on my tongue and close my eyes. She breathes in and stands up very quickly. I say I'm sorry for becoming too familiar with her. She says, "Sorry? You are so kind and I needed someone to hold and share my hurt. You understand what it means to have someone you love in your heart but not in your arms. You are a good man."

I slowly move away as to not let her think I am leaving. She walks away slowly and says it is time for her to start the morning fire and get the dough ready for breakfast bread since it has been rising all night. I stand there feeling satisfied that the logs to heat the house and cook our meal are from the wood I chopped.

I sit down in the parlor and begin to smell both the fire burning and the bread baking as I look out the window and see the sun over yonder and the sky starting to brighten as a light snow falls on the already thick, snow-covered ground.

Dr. Nott's Concerns about War

Life has not been easy with the talk of war, which leads to debating and fighting between our Southern students and our Northern students and our household being down one man, Moses Viney for almost two years. As the president and pastoral leader of this college, I am overwhelmed by the day-to-day conflicts and bad news on my campus and off the campus.

Local abolitionists are working in cities on both the east and west side of the campus—Troy and Syracuse—with Schenectady in the middle. I have heard that an escaped slave named Frederick Douglass has been speaking in Troy and was surprised when I found out that he was from the same Maryland county as Moses himself. He speaks well and people listen to him.

Although I understand the mission of abolitionists to end slavery, I do hope that our government can determine a compromise so that the Southern states' economic status is not compromised. Our Southern boys are good students and a government compromise may affect their families' incomes.

Moses has learned from the boys in college and picked up on what they were learning. Moses speaks well, too, as he tried to learn more new words every day. I liked to watch him when a visitor or student would say an uncommon word. I knew Moses did not know the word, and I watched him repeat the word and the sentence under his breath.

Soon thereafter, I'd hear him repeating the word in a sentence to me or the Mrs. He is a very smart man. He is a very caring man. And without him in the house I see his absence taking its toll on Mrs. Nott.

I am trying my best to work with that most stubborn slave owner Murphy. He asks for such outrageous sums of money for a man he should not morally own. My grandson, Clarkson Potter, continues to try to bargain down this stupid man who is demanding sums of money that are outrageous.

With the talk of a war between the North and the South, he may want to be more agreeable, so I'm sending my grandson to correspond with Murphy one more time. It's been almost two years without Moses, and I know his wife suffers so much without him and his husbandly duties.

My bones and muscles are getting stiffer by the day, though Mrs. Nott is trying her best to help. She has such small delicate hands that she cannot push and pull the muscles as well as Moses can. She and Anna have helped me handle the stairs, though one night we all had a laugh when it felt like one of them was pushing while the other was pulling me up the stairs. Although I laughed, pride got in the way as I yelled unnecessarily at the cat that got underfoot and we all landed on the floor.

I also miss my talks with Moses, especially when he talked of the students. He was more understanding of the young students than I since he was closer to their age. I would get very frustrated when a student would miss church service, or didn't understand a good sermon, or was caught in the wrong section of the city with a moral misdeed.

Moses would listen well and present another perspective of the student's behavior that I would not have considered. Sometimes he would let me know some difficulty a young lad might have been having with his family or with other students. Though I made sure each student received a fair and just punishment for their pranks, I know I might have been harsher if I hadn't considered what Moses brought to the conversation.

I also know that the students respect Moses almost as much as they respect me. He has a special relationship with them, boys from both the North and the South. If he is present in the room, they nod to him and then step forward to shake my hand. I'm quite sure they see in him what I see, a man of integrity, who will do an honest day's work and more in order to be of right mind with his soul. I am also quite pleased to see that Moses is a regular church-going man, though I think that Anna has been the catalyst for this.

He rides our cart carefully and does not rush us to chapel, but I sense his eagerness as the horse canters out the front gates to his church where his wife awaits. He must miss her so and regret the time that has set back his want for a family. I have decided to bring Moses back to the States and hope for an agreement with Murphy. It will take a few days for a message to get to Moses and then a few days for the journey back to Schenectady. I know this is taking a chance on his life, but I think that my grandson will be able to close a deal soon for I've given him a fair amount of money to bargain with.

I believe that with the talk of war, Murphy might consider that it would be better to sell a slave that you no longer control than to keep a slave that is not helping you make good money on the plantation. I pray that Murphy does not hear of Moses' return to the States until after a deal is made.

Mrs. Nott Contemplates Life Without Eliphalet

Eliphalet continues to try so hard to handle the college, the public and his own health. As his wife, I know I'm blessed to have him in my life, but he is so much older than I. He is getting weaker every day, but does have some good days although seemingly more bad days. I've been working so very hard corresponding with the Head Mistress of my new school, the Utica Female Academy, that I may have neglected some of my marriage duties. Eliphalet is more than thirty years older than I am, but when I first met him he was a spry, dignified man who supported my work of establishing strong educational facilities for young women.

I met him in Utica shortly after his wife died. We had many talks and walks before I realized I was very much in love with him. I think he took his time to ask for my hand, about five years, because he thought I would not be in agreement. My work at the Utica Female Academy was going very successfully as did the other schools for girls I had established in Schenectady and in Nassau, New York.

This school was much needed in the area since the girls had very little opportunity to get a decent education. When Eliphalet and I married, I did not have to worry: the school was strong, had many young women attending, and had good quality teachers. As I left for Schenectady as his wife, he felt the young men at the college would be very accepting of me as would the local politicians. He also felt he needed someone with my education and upbringing to help with important decisions of the college that would be beneficial to the boys.

As I got to know some of the political influences of the college and the country, Eliphalet took pleasure in including me in decisions of the college. My worries were about the expectations and responsibilities placed on Eliphalet, especially their influence on his health and well-being. There are times when I must now interrupt and end discussions he has with colleagues in order to ensure he is rested and ready for other responsibilities that he has to attend to. I try never to interrupt his conversations with the students since I truly feel Eliphalet gets stronger after having discussions and sometimes debates with students.

He is always challenging their intellectual capabilities or he is chastising them for inappropriate behavior. All of his conversations with the young boys lead him to have more energy and thought-provoking ideas about the future of the world.

I must now think of Eliphalet's future with me. Living in the South Colonnade with him has been at times adventurous and at other times lacking in privacy. I am as in love with my husband as I have ever been because he treats me as his equal and appreciates my opinion, but now I feel more like his protector.

We have talked about getting Moses back to Union College and paying whatever the next offer that is posed by that notorious Murphy. We have also decided to bring Moses back quietly because his skills are needed by Eliphalet even though we do not have a confirmed conclusion on his freedom.

I do believe Eliphalet misses Moses, not just as his driver, nor as solely his helpmate with his rheumatism, but also as his confidante. Eliphalet can become very sullen when he is in his most pain, but he does not share this with anyone. Moses' intuition notifies him of the ailments and he instantly knows how to handle Eliphalet. That is what Eliphalet misses, someone with the instincts to know when he should stop or slow down his work to rest with a cup of tea, or how to massage his finger joints when they have stiffened so he can get his paperwork completed. I can assist Eliphalet with decisions on the best education we can offer our students.

Moses assists with helping Eliphalet be physically able to complete projects, be fully present for meetings with high-powered men, and in handling the pranks that some of the boys get into.

I also have to consider our future together and I'm thinking a house would be better for Eliphalet and me to live in rather than the Colonnade. Moses and Anna live in a small cottage behind our home. They are able to leave the students and have a private space beyond the reaches of the boys. I have brought up the subject of a house for the president with the Board and Eliphalet.

I have looked into the best way to bring up the subject of funds for building a President's House, not so big as a mansion, but a true presence on the campus that stays within the gates of the campus and respects the design of our campus architectural plan. A house will allow more time away from the almost twenty-four hour existence with the students. And if something should happen to Eliphalet, I will still have a place to live, for it would be difficult to justify a widow staying in the dormitory with twenty men in the facility. I must continue to consider these things within these fleeting seasons of life.

Chapter Twenty-five

Bidding Goodbye to Canada

The ground has softened now that the weather is warm and the snow has melted into the soil to provide a soft, muddy layer. The winter was harsh on my body—my ears burned all the time even with lard on them and my hands ached through to the bone. Although it is still cold in the morning even with spring in the air, the work warms up the body and the only thing that remains cold are my hands.

I've learned from the other workers to put paper on the inside of my boots and wear two pairs of socks to keep my feet warm. I tuck my wool and itchy but warm long-johns and my outside pants into my boots as well and tuck both my under and outside shirts into the waist pants. I wear many layers to hold in my body warmth and keep out the cold. And I take off layers as I get warm from the good, hard work.

There is one other colored person working this field who bothers me; his name is Buddy. We don't speak much after our first talk when I arrived. He is a stubborn man. He is an escaped slave from Georgia. He came up to Canada five years or so ago with his brother.

When I met him, I told him my story of Dr. Nott paying for my freedom and was expecting him to understand. He instead took off at me saying, "What you mean, a white man is going to buy back your freedom? Why you here then? Here in Canada, we are free, but we are not free. We keep lookin' back hoping no one is still following us. You know they can come up here and take us back in the night against our will even though we supposed to be free. My master not come up here. He too fat and lazy. But no one wants to buy our freedom to go to the States; no one is out there looking out for us. We can never go back. I want to go back home and see my people. I want to hug my pa. My ma's dead and my pa told me and my brother to escape. My pa was too old to run, but we could run to freedom. So we planned a runaway from the plantation and here we are."

"You have a white man willing to buy your freedom and you run anyway to Canada. You leave your wife behind waitin' for you. If she pretty, you know she gonna find someone else, she ain't waitin' fo' you. What kind of man are you?"

As he talked, I was getting as hot as the hell the preacher talks about! I wanted to hurt him, like he just hurt me, but instead I told him, "You best stop talkin' bout what you don't know. I'll be going back soon, you hear."

And with that, we don't have much more to say. I worked hard that day to let go the anger and I prayed. I prayed every night on my knees before going to sleep. I learned to pray by watching Dr. Nott and Anna. We don't pray on our knees on the plantation. The first night that I worked for Dr. Nott, I helped him with his nightshirt as he made his way to the bed.

Now, we on the plantation worked so hard that at night all we did was lie down and fall right off to sleep. When Dr. Nott got down on his knees, I had almost rushed over to help him up. But he folded his hands on the bed and bowed his head, so I just stood by the washbasin stand. He started talking out loud to nobody, but it was clear that he was talking to somebody and it was God. Sometimes, he would talk like there'd be a person that was right next to him and sometimes it was in a whisper, but you could hear the words. I always stayed by the door after that to hear him say his prayers, as he called it. Although many times I couldn't hear all the words, I know it made him feel better to pray before he went to bed. He also prayed over his meals and led prayer in church, but it was Anna who got me to praying.

On our first night together before we even touched each other, she placed a rug by the edge of the bed, took my hand and got down on her knees by our bed. I joined her only doing what I saw Dr. Nott do. She then started talking to God, in a soft but determined voice.

I remember she asked God to watch over her brother and his family and her church. She also prayed for those who did not have food or a home. Then she elbowed me to say something. I asked God to watch over my ma and pa and brothers and sisters and all the people on the plantation and to set them free.

I didn't know what else to say and then it came to me, "God, please watch over my Anna. She is the most precious thing I have."

Then I knew to end by saying, "In Jesus' name. Amen," and she said, "Amen" at the same time. I say that now at the end of every day and at the end of every prayer. That night, after my conversation with Buddy, I said it again, only that time I said it with a lot more meaning 'cause I didn't want Buddy's words to be true. Anna is the most precious thing I have and I pray she stays true to me.

That was last winter and here I am, still in Canada. I'm not worried about my Anna; she is a good woman. As I plowed the dirt and mud, I saw one of the workers running out to the field towards us. It can't be suppertime, or the bell would ring. He was running so fast he kicked up dirt and mud. He was out of breath but yelling my name and telling me to go to the house right away.

At first, I just stood there, then I dropped the reins to the horse and plow and began to run towards the house not wanting to waste time unhitching the horse to take me back to the big house. My mind was running too. Was there something wrong at the house? Now why would they call only me? Was there news from New York? Could Anna be hurt? Was someone dead or sick? They never called me in from the fields before.

This can't be good. I run faster until I'm on the porch in the doorway. Bessie was looking at me as I tried to breathe more slowly. She looked at my boots, covered in mud. She wiped her hands on her apron and untied my boots 'cause I can't move as I coughed and inhaled deeply.

As she did this quickly, she said, "The mail came and Mr. Palemont is in the library. All I knows is that he got a letter from New York and he up and yelled to get you in here right-away."

I kicked off my boots, took the hat off my head but not the coat off my back! I walked swiftly to the library.

Mr. Palemont said, "Have a seat, Moses. There's a letter here for you."

I looked him in the eye, stayed standing, and he said nothing. Still standing, I began to moan like when my ma moaned when she lost a baby too small to cry. I moaned a low noise that came from deep within my belly, not knowing why. I just knew the news ain't gonna be good. He leaned over and grabbed me and shook my shoulders and said, "It's not that awful. It's not bad news and it's not good news."

I looked up and asked slowly, "What does the letter say, sir?"

Mr. Palemont looked me in the eyes: "Dr. Nott would like for you to return to the States, but the decision is up to you. There are some details and some concerns. You are not a free man and you will not be one when you return. Dr. Nott has not yet worked out a deal for your freedom, but he sent his grandson to your old master one more time. He thinks that with the talk of a war in the States you may not be worth much now and the master may want to make a decent deal.

"I don't know what's going on in the States, but I don't think a war where there's killing is going to help the country. But I'm from Canada and we wouldn't settle our disagreements that way. We just don't believe in slavery anymore so we voted it out. It's just not good for you colored people and you deserve to be free and make money to feed your own families."

I looked at him still not understanding him: "If he hasn't bought my freedom, why should I go back?"

Mr. Palemont said, "I think he needs you Moses. Dr. Nott is leaving the decision up to you. He would like for you to come back and he would find ways to protect you. I think he needs you back since he is an older man since you left. He sent his grandson back south and hopes that you will only be in New York a few months before a deal is finally settled.

"He said the decision is up to you. Take your chance and go back to the States without freedom, or live here to maintain your freedom. You are a good worker and I'd keep you on if you decided to stay. I would also understand your need to go back as well."

The room was silent. Bessie and Lok were at the door along with two other field hands and Buddy. Mr. Palemont pointed to the couch and told me to sit down, which I obliged 'cause I think I might have fallen down at that moment. I felt everyone's eyes on me. If I don't go back now, I still have a job here and can help get the fields planted this spring. If I go back, I may have to always look over my shoulder to see if there was someone following me to bring me back to slavery.

I've felt that feeling too many times since I left the plantation. If I stay, I will always have a roof over my head and food in my stomach. But it is not Anna's food, and I won't have her in my arms, the smell of her hair, the touch of her skin next to mine, her cheek on my chest, her arms around my neck.

I looked up at Mr. Palemont, "Sir, you and your family have been so kind to take me in and put me to work. Bessie, you have become a good friend to me, and Lok, although you are a quiet one, I have learned some things about your people, and I always appreciate your presence. But I must go back. I'll take my chances and go back 'cause I miss my wife and my work with the Notts. I can no longer run away anymore. I won't have my freedom, but I don't have my freedom now. If I did, Anna would be in my arms and we would have a family. My children will be free even if I am not. I must go back, you do understand this?"

Mr. Palemont smiled and nodded, while Bessie and now six other field hands were clapping and whooping out loud. I stood up to Mr. Palemont and shook his hand in thanks. I walked over to Bessie and gave her a big hug and kiss on the cheek and watched her round cheeks blush a brilliant red. I walked over to Lok. He bowed. I bowed and all was said in this little gesture.

I said to the field hands, "Come on, men. I'm not leaving until we get the whole ground plowed so that I leave knowing I did my share of work 'round here."

As I walked out the door, Mr. Palemont said, "I'll make arrangements for a train to take you back to the States within the week. Bessie, we need a cake for supper tonight. We've got something to celebrate."

I walked past Buddy who had his hat in his hand. He put out his hand to me and I shook it. He grabbed my elbow and pulled me closer to him and said, "You will surely be free now. You will be free, Moses, and your wife will be by your side."

And with that, I was satisfied to be going home, yes home. Schenectady is and always will be my home 'cause my heart is there, my Anna. We can begin to raise a family and continue our work with Dr. Nott and his Mrs. at Union College.

Chapter Twenty-six

Freedom?

As I said goodbye to the Palemonts knowing that they were good people, I realized I would miss them and would probably never see them again. I boarded the train which smelled of coal and steam, and they were now good smells. Miss. Bessie and Mr. Palemont were the only ones at the station to say good-bye.

Bessie gave me a hug and said, "Don't you go and make too many babies; give her a rest now and then. I know you missed her, but she may need a break from your good lovin'." We all laughed. Mr. Palemont shook my hand and handed me the rest of my pay.

"Tell ol' Eliphalet I sends my regards."

As the bell whistled I hopped on the train, which was movin' by then, and waved until the tracks turned and I could not see them anymore.

As the train crossed from Canada to the States, my hair got on ends on my arms. I wasn't scared, just worried. Without true freedom here, I will never be free. I do hope Dr. Nott now has some news on my behalf. The train ride seemed faster going home and as we pulled into Schenectady, I hopped off hoping to be greeted by Anna or someone.

No one was at the station, not one person I recognized. So I started my walk up Liberty Street towards Union Street. Liberty Street, to think my first walk back in Schenectady was on Liberty Street. My step became faster when I realized I was home and as I approached Union Street I was running, up and onto the campus and there was our home. I walked inside and it smelled of fresh bread, but Anna was not there. I called out and realized she must be working for the Notts.

I headed over to their home and walked in the back door. I saw the cook on one side of the butcher table and my Anna on the other. The cook gave out a scream as my Anna looked up from the table and ran over and hugged me. She was crying and laughing and huggin' and kissin' all over my face.

Oh, what a pleasure moment I will not forget until the day I die. I picked her up in my arms and we sat on the chair with her on my lap. She said she didn't know if or when I was coming back:

"Dr. Nott had sent a letter up north, but we never received a letter back. We weren't sure whether you got the letter and didn't know when or if you were coming back."

Mrs. Nott burst into the room to see what the commotion was about and looked at us, the cook with her hand over her mouth and me in the chair with Anna right there on my lap. I almost stood up but knew Anna would slide right off onto the floor, so I just sat there. Mrs. Nott yelled, "Eliphalet, you come in here quick as you can. Come on."

Then she turned in the doorway to grab his hand. He walked in and said, "Praise be to the Father, you have returned, my son."

He called me son. Now, I know he didn't mean it in the birth way, but he did mean it in some way. Anna stood up so as I could stand and walk over to him. We did not shake hands and for the first time in my life I hugged a white man. But what was most important was that he hugged me back. He hugged me, a colored man, who he was trying to make free.

And from then on forward I would give my life for Dr. Nott as surely as I would for my Anna. I would do it and not feel beholdin' to him, but would do it because he has a special place in my heart that will always be there.

That afternoon I spent time with Dr. Nott in the library talking about the deal. He had sent his grandson with money to bargain for between $100 and $200. He said, "If Murphy was a fair-minded man, he should take $100, but if he was a greedy man he would take much more. That's why I limited the amount. I think that with the talk of war, Murphy don't want to be bothered having a slave who don't want to be bothered with him. So I think this time he would be more willing to negotiate a fair and good price. Your freedom is worth a fair and good price, not some outrageous amount that would make me a fool. 'Cause if truth was to call, no one would have to buy anyone's freedom, since all men should be free."

As I listened to Dr. Nott, I realized he was much older than he was two years ago. His hair was much whiter and thinner and he had much more difficulty standing and sitting. Since it was evening, I helped him to dress into his nightshirt and watched him ever so slowly kneel to pray. As he closed his eyes, I closed mine and thanked the Lord for guiding me to this man of righteousness who took me in and now my Anna. And I whispered:

"Watch over him and his wife, Mrs. Nott, dear Lord. And please consider Dr. Nott's words carefully. All men should be free, and that includes me. As we thank our good Lord. Amen."

After I helped him to bed under the sheets that Mrs. Nott heated with the bed warmer, he asked me not to massage his legs. He said it could wait until his morning bath because Anna would be waiting for me on my first night home. So, I thanked him, closed the door and headed swiftly to my home and my Anna, who would be waiting with supper for us. I walked into my home.

She looked at me and said, "Boots off first, sit in the chair." Then she walked over and placed a pair of black slippers on my feet. They were brand new and soft. I asked how she could afford a pair. She said, "Dr. Nott continued to pay me half your wages since I was doing half your work. So I set some of the money aside to get you something special. Mrs. Nott helped me think about them 'cause she said Dr. Nott becomes relaxed when he has his slippers on. Now you relax and I'll fetch your supper. You must be starving. I didn't have time to make your favorites, so I whipped up some chicken and your favorite biscuits, and for dessert, lemon butter cake. Those were the only things I had time to make with you surprising us and all."

As she brought over the dishes, I just sat and smelled the food and as my mouth began to water I shoveled, yes, shoveled the food into my mouth as if I hadn't eaten since I left. Yes, Bessie was a good cook, but this was better because Anna had made it. She ate with me but not as fast. When I was done, she began to clear the table, but I stopped her. I took her hand and placed it around my waist.

Then I held her tight and knew she was holding her breath. I looked into her face and began kissing it all over. She melted into my arms, soft tears falling down her cheeks. She opened her mouth for my kiss and as I kissed her deeply, I carried her into our bedroom. It was time to start working on building our family, our family of free children in America. And she was willing to begin as well. In the moonlight before we started, she pointed out the window at our North Star.

I said, "Our North Star has brought me back to you my Anna, for me to stay, always."

Moses Viney in his later years as a free man at Union College. Union College Library Special Collections

Chapter Twenty-seven

Building the President's House

Now that I am back I'm noticing more changes. Dr. Nott is in a lot more pain, walking more slowly and his hair is much greyer. Mrs. Nott looks tired, but according to Anna she seems to be less worried now that I am back. And Anna is set on starting a family; it would be nice to have my children be free. Ah, freedom. My pa would be proud to know his grandchildren will be free children, the first free babies in our family as far as I can tell.

Imagine giving birth and not worrying that someone would sell your babies, or knowing that your child is yours and not your master's child. Our children will be free and will get an education, learning good English and wearing shoes as soon as they could walk.

Anna says she likes my new accent. I don't hear any difference, but she says I have one. She has been so good to me since I got back. She is a very caring wife, always pleasing me and looking after my needs, but she says she is worried about Mrs. Nott.

"Mrs. Nott is a much younger woman and Dr. Nott is not getting any younger. Who will take care of Mrs. Nott when he is gone? Surely, she could remarry, but where will she live, where will she go if he dies first? He is more likely to go before her."

I had not thought of this. I was so worried about my freedom, and not for the people who were going to help guarantee my freedom.

This morning I woke up with my Anna in my arms smelling like sleep and curled up on my chest. I looked out the window and realized the sun was just about to rise. I slipped out of bed to dress and start my day with President Nott, hoping today we would have news from Maryland and also determined to talk with Dr. Nott.

When I got to Dr. Nott's room, he was already awake but not out of bed, just sitting up looking out the window. His walk has grown feeble, so that he walks now more slowly in his gait and with more difficulty. His face has grown full of lines and deep crevices. He was thinner and he stooped over, but his eyes and sense of his surroundings were still bright and alert.

He greeted me with the usual: "Morning, Moses. It is a fine day God has prepared."

He said that most mornings whether it was a fine day or not. I helped him out of his night dressing and prepared him to wash up. I went to put the kettle on the fire and poured warm water into the basin. I washed his back and arms while he took care of his other parts. I noticed his arms and legs were thinner and stiffer.

As he took a seat, I grasped his hands and placed them in the basin of warm water and began to massage each finger, which now felt like bones with thin skin holding them in. I rubbed up his wrist and arms until I reached his back. I worked hard but without hurting him and I felt him relaxing as I rubbed his shoulders and back. I won't work on his legs until the eve, after a long day on his feet.

As I helped him dress, I asked him how Mrs. Nott has been feeling since I was gone. He said:

"Mrs. Nott prayed for you every day as I did. That was a long time away and she and your Mrs. worked well together to help get our day started. I do worry about her, but she's a woman who can take care of herself when times are hard. You know she started schools for women, and she has a good head for money. But I think she is weary of living in these halls with the students. We might be making some decisions about living here. You and Anna leave the young men to go to your own private home. We had a lovely home down in the Stockade, but now that we are on this upper campus, we've been living with the students.

"I get to know them better, but I think the Mrs. needs some time away from them for privacy with me. She's been talking about establishing a new President's house. At first I argued against it, but what right do I have to force my wife to live where she doesn't want to? It's not right at all."

As he stepped into his shoes so I could button them, he held my shoulder and I felt his fragile hold.

"Urania deserves to have a house be more like a home. She loves these boys, but I think they may be a wear on her and me. And there are days when I am apt to agree especially since you've been gone. I think you had a presence with them especially when they misbehaved. When you would bring them to me, they had a sense of remorse for their behavior and knew how to plead their case. Since you've been gone, they come in cowering and in fear or they come in angry and defensive. It is good to have you back, my boy. You are so good for the boys and, if I had to be honest, you are so good for me and Mrs. Nott."

With that he was fully dressed and we headed to his library to start the day.

These few days in the States have been a blessing and a curse. I am back with my beloved Anna and we are still trying to carry a child. I've watched Anna with her nieces and nephews and she would make a wonderful mother. But alas, God has not blessed us with any news. Anna is still attentive to my needs, but is now less tense settling on putting this problem into God's hands.

So, every eve as the stars shine and the North Star glows, I get on my knees and ask for three things: to have Anna with child as soon as God is able, to have my freedom from the young Master Murphy so that I don't have to look over my shoulder for him to take me back and to bless the Notts as they work with these young boys to get them a good education.

This morning, which was not particular to any other morn, Anna was over at the Nott's helping prepare breakfast while I got dressed and then I went over to assist Dr. Nott with his day. Dr. Nott and I went into Schenectady City for a few meetings that he had with local business folks. All was going well until about noon, when one of the stable boys came running down the street as we were getting back into the carriage. He was out of breath so it took a while for him to come out and say what was on his mind.

"Dr. Nott, you got a telegraph from your grandson. Mrs. Nott says, get home right away."

And with that, I snapped the whip right over the ears of the horses and we headed back to campus with a quicker pace than the horses were used to.

Upon entering the South Lodges, Dr. Nott, who seemed to have lost his limp as he rushed inside, asked for Urania to meet him in the library and he asked me to stay. The messenger, who had been waiting in the parlor, was called in and handed Dr. Nott the telegram. Dr. Nott fumbled with his glasses, took a deep breath, and with his stiffened fingers opened up the folds of the letter. Still standing behind his huge oak desk, he fixed his glasses on his nose and looked down as we watched his eyes go from left to right on each line of the words.

He wasn't saying anything, just moving his eyes. He put the letter down on his desk, took off his glasses and sat down in his chair. We stood, Mrs. Nott and I, with the messenger in the shadows of the books on the shelves. Dr. Nott pulled out his kerchief from his pocket and cleaned off his glasses and looked up at me.

"Well, Mr. Viney," he said with a slight quiver in his lower lip, "how does it feel to be free?"

I reached for the arm of the couch and could do nothing but sit down, leaving Mrs. Nott standing, which was not proper. But I could not stand any longer. Dr. Nott repeated:

"How does it feel, my son, to be free?"

I quickly found my place, stood up and nodded in apology to Mrs. Nott for sitting down whilst she stood up, and I said to him with the only words I could say, "Dr. Nott, Mrs. Nott, I feel much obliged for your generosity. I feel like my heart is going to burst with laughter and with tears. I feel like a new man."

And as I said this, I knew I had become too familiar with Mrs. Nott in the room and bowed my head and looked at my shoes.

Dr. Nott said, "The free Mr. Moses Viney, hold your head up high. For you are feeling something you never knew all the days of your life. What you said comes from your heart and that, my boy, is better sometimes than what comes from your head."

And we smiled, we all smiled. And I heard the eager footsteps of Anna running up the steps. As she joined us, Mrs. Nott said, "Come on in, woman, and hug your free husband."

Chapter Twenty-eight

Free in America

To be back in the States these few months knowing I can walk out my front door and never experience the fear of enslavement feels wonderful every day. I have a purpose on this Earth, to have free children with my loving wife, Anna, and work for a man who bought my freedom, which I will do until my last breath of life—not because I am indebted to him, but because he and I are now on equal footing.

My work is good work for this college and his work is good work for this college and the two of us will use our best skills to make these students better people in what I fear will be troubled times ahead for all.

At home, Anna and I are doing our duty to try to build our own family. At work, Dr. Nott's health is getting weaker and Mrs. Nott sees this. She has completed building a house for them, which is a fine thing to do and has already made it easier on them both. Students don't just drop in on him during times when he is to be resting.

And Mrs. Nott who has spent much time on improving Dr. Nott's health has had some time to focus on decorating the house; she needs this break.

Here in the States--and I got used to saying "the States" after living in Canada--we are at war. The Civil War has begun and we are saddened. But we must fight the good fight. So many young people are heading off to fight a war between our states so that more colored people will be free. Many of the young boys from college are going off to war, too. Some of them are even leading the colored troops into action.

Who would have thought that white men would fight for the freedom of colored people, that these white students would march side-by-side with our colored troops? I hope that soon all this death and dying of soldiers will end and we will all be free. But right now my main concern is for Dr. Nott. He is troubled by the war, the politics and the campus finances.

Mrs. Nott is helping him make the best decisions for the college. I've had to offer more massages for his legs and arms and he is grateful for that. More recently, I've had to carry him upstairs to his bedroom for he can no longer manage the staircase. He is still a strong man, both mentally and physically. I feel his strong arms around my neck as we both manage what would be an embarrassment for some.

Dr. Nott is grateful to still show and share his strength in wisdom to his students and other very powerful politicians who come to him for advice. I can also tell that he has something on his mind, but we've not had an occasion to talk with the daily schedule of work he's been having.

Meetings with William Seward, a former student and a politician, and other leaders have been long and hard on him, but he seems to get up the gumption to sit up at length and discuss matters for hours. At the end of the day, he allows all the pain to come forward and we work together to ease the aches. This is when we talk, in the quiet of the evening, after dinner and before his bedtime.

Tonight I know there is something on his mind, so I just decide to ask him if there's something he wants to talk about.

Dr. Nott, who is half lying on bed and half sitting up as I rub his arms, looks up at me, coughs, and says, "Well, Moses, we've been through a lot these past few years. I have shared more things with you than I have with my own wife sometimes. You know we cannot do what we need for these students without you and Anna's work here at the college. You also know that as long as I'm taking breath on this good Earth, you will have a position here.

"There is something I've been meaning to tell you and it might just be the right time."

Well, at this point, I was so confused I had no idea what he was talking about, and I was worried. Dr. Nott straightened out his nightshirt and took my hands off his arms and placed them in his.

He began, "This war may go on for many years, and I want you to know I have secured your freedom papers with the family attorneys. In addition, my health has not been right in many years and it weighs on Mrs. Nott's shoulders. Therefore, after I'm gone, 'cause I'm sure going to go before you, I will make sure you and your family are taken care of.

"But I want assurance from you that you will take care of my wife as long as she needs the both of you. Can you swear to that nature?"

I looked at this man, whose hair is so very white and thin, his arms are slightly strong, but his legs are only skin and bones. And I believe the feeling I'm feeling is pure love for a man who cares so much about me, my family and his wife that he wants us to care for each other after he's gone.

I look deep into his eyes, maybe into his soul, and say, "I will always be there for whatever Mrs. Nott needs from me. I believe in the afterlife that you will watch over us as my brother and my friend— part of the heavenly host that will do spiritual warfare on our behalf."

A Home, Freedom, and Family

The war has been raging for nearly four years now. Many of our students have gone off to fight for the freedom of slaves, but I have to say many more have put off their education to fight for their Southern families. In this war, it is hard to realize that some of our students may be fighting or killing each other.

Dr. Nott feels this every day even while paying some attention to the decorating of the new house, which I say is fit for a king. The new house looks like a mansion; it has stairs leading up to columns to a grand entrance. The front foyer is set with a magnificent stairwell at least six feet wide leading up to bedrooms. At the base of the stairs to the right is President Nott's library, with a fire to warm his achy joints and shelving for his many books. Dr. Nott is a pastor and also an inventor.

He decided to place his invention, the Nott Stove, throughout the house in each fireplace. This stove saves the college money because it is designed to use coal, which is better than wood or charcoal. On the other side of the library is the parlor, with the comfort of a fireplace and an open area to the dining room; it is a very welcoming and warm room. The dining room is large enough for Mrs. Nott to hosts many events. It is a grand house and looks good at the entrance of the college lawns.

In the new house, it is now easier for Dr. Nott to get around and for Mrs. Nott to entertain at tea. With Dr. Nott's library on the first floor, I now have to carry him upstairs to the bedroom quarters to get him to bed. The wide staircase makes this task easier. He likes to be in the library warmed by his Nott Stove; he is proud of this work but is humble enough to credit God with the glory.

"All I have and am is due to my Lord and Saviour, Jesus the Christ," he says.

He is able to come down the stairs at a slow pace and, at times, we all work together to make him comfortable: me with his private necessities, Anna with organizing the household and Mrs. Nott, who listens to his wants and needs and lets us know how best to assist him.

Anna and I have been trying for years to have a family, but it is not meant to be. We have settled on the fact that these young students are our children. They treat us with respect, ask for advice, keep up with their school and religious studies, and are well-trained in their manners.

It is rumored that the war will end this year and we pray for a peaceful ending, with slaves feeling their freedom and ex-slaves living in comfort and without fear of being taken back into the darkness of slavery.

Dr. Nott has been so very worried about the finances. He has been in and out of meetings and court fighting against those who question his integrity. He receives telegrams every day. Our students are not attending school due to the war. Before I returned, we had over four hundred students attending Union College. They were bright and energized with no fear of war.

It is now 1865 and we barely have two hundred students. Their fees help cover the costs of running the college and all our salaries, including the professors. Although he suffered from pain, Nott was troubled by the country's war and prayed for its ending. Dr. Nott met with many dignitaries, like Seward and other political and religious leaders trying to understand the war.

But President Nott was suffering every day from what the doctor called strokes. Some days Nott would be able to hold a conversation about state affairs and some days his mind would be back to his early days.

On one of the worst days for Dr. Nott, we received a telegram. Mrs. Nott was worried, so she read the news silently while standing at the door. She took a seat after reading it and looked up and simply said, "The war is over."

That was all she said as she looked up the stairs to where Dr. Nott was hurting from the pain. She proceeded upstairs with me following. As she stood over his bed, she read him the news and with that Dr. Nott asked to get dressed and wanted tea downstairs. He knew our boys, our students, would be back.

Mrs. Nott and I were delighted that he understood and felt better with the news. And then it hit me, we just received the news that the war was over. The North has won and the last of the big Southern armies surrendered. President Lincoln had worked hard to keep the Union of states together, which was his main goal, with the notion of freeing the slaves a priority.

In the end, Lincoln's mission to keep the state of the Union together also ended slavery in America. Our sons were coming home and for some families their daughters who were nursing our wounded would be coming home, too. Maybe with the end of the war, the college's finances would get better and more students would come back to college.

The End of an Era

It's been a rough year. The violent shooting death of President Lincoln took a toll on Dr. Nott and on me, too. Mr. Lincoln had freed all of the slaves and someone took his life because of this. The weak scoundrel shot an unarmed man as he sat watching a play—the coward.

Lincoln's assassination was heartbreaking for the United States. But on the same day the assassins were killing Lincoln, some of them went to the home of

William Seward, by this time he was the Secretary of State's, and tried to kill him. William Henry Seward was an 1820 graduate of Union College and the stabbing he received from the attempt permanently maimed him for life.

As Secretary of State, he is a very important leader of our country, but he was strong and lived through the attack. Dr. Nott took the news hard and has been more feeble ever since. Although he's had a number of strokes, there are times when he is with us enough to talk and wants to learn news. Dr. Nott was very close to Mr. Seward; they talked often. Mrs. Nott has been helping with the running of the college, though we are not supposed to talk about that. She meets regularly with the other leaders of the college; she is a smart woman and they seem to respect her thinking.

It has been hard for me for I have had mixed feelings this winter. Christmas was a blessing to be excited for the holiday. But it was a hard winter with the weather aching Dr. Nott's bones. I have been massaging his legs, arms and back every day. He curls up in a ball, suffering days and nights. I must say that there are days when I am torn up and exhausted because it is so difficult watching this once strong man hurting so much and losing weight. His skin on his hands is so thin and wrinkled that I can see the veins.

These hands and arms have skin so loose that it stretches and is harder to massage without meat on the bones. When I massage, I hear his breath ease as I rub with warm oils. I talk to him about the goings-on of the college 'cause I know he is listening and he likes to hear about the students' pranks and how they are doing on their studies.

As I turn him over, for he is not able to turn himself, and start with his shoulders, I notice some sores on his hip side. I stop to look at the open skin area and put liniment on it that Mrs. Nott got from the doctor. It burns him and I see his face wrinkle up, but he doesn't complain. I ease him onto his belly and begin with his shoulders again, working down his ribs, making sure I don't press so hard that it hurts him, but not too soft that it's not helping. I share with him how strong Mrs. Nott is and how she is working hard and I share how the locals are building more churches for colored folks and giving us education for our children.

As I work my way down to his long, thin legs, I begin to talk about his teaching me: how I learned to pray on my knees, how I watched him handle powerful men by being calm and smart and always looking them in the eye so they had to respond to him with respect, how I learned new words and how sometimes I think he said a new word so I could learn it fast.

I talk about how good he is to Anna and me. We have a house now and I am no longer a slave because of his generosity. I tell him that I never felt obliged to stay here, but I felt that we, he and I, were more than just boss and worker. He is a friend and a teacher and I love him like a brother. He watched over me in my desperate need and I have and will always watch over him, even now when he is most in need of my help.

I turn him back over and tuck his arms under the blanket to keep him warm. Normally, he would be up in his library 'til late into the night, but this eve the sun has set early and darkness came early. I lift the covers off his legs 'cause he doesn't like tight blankets on his skin—they are too rough. Then, I look him in the face. You can see that he's aged, but you can also see wisdom behind those eyes. He blinks and slowly closes them and I know he's near the end. I call downstairs for Mrs. Nott who is having tea and biscuits. She comes upstairs in a hurry, sensing something is wrong and Anna is right behind her. Anna comes in and takes his wrist to check for a beat and she says it will not be long.

Mrs. Nott sits in the chair next to his bed, while I sit by his feet. Normally, we would never be alone like this, but we don't live by most proper rules anymore because Mrs. Nott and I have to work together to comfort Dr. Nott. As the new dawn rises, Mrs. Nott is leaning over his face as she kisses him one last time and President Nott takes his last rattling breath.

She sobs, heaving shoulders, and I leave the room to give her the privacy she deserves to have with her husband. In a few minutes, she calls me back in, tells me to take care of him while she sends the message that Eliphalet Nott, President of Union College, has died peacefully on campus.

As she leaves, I wash Dr. Nott to prepare him for his final resting place and dress him in his best suit. As I do this, I hear the voices of students outside his window. I am not sure how many students and faculty and staff I see, but they are saying The Lord's Prayer and Bible verses while some are crying.

It is now that I sit in the chair next to his bed and I cry many tears--tears of gratefulness for knowing this man of integrity, honesty, and a heart filled with goodness for all. I cry tears of worry for Mrs. Nott who loved him so much and never allowed their years of difference to sway her affection for him. I cry tears of hurt and pain for I have lost a dear friend, a kind pastor and spiritual leader.

The week is taken up preparing for the funeral. Many great leaders and local folks and students will be attending. We are busy, so busy, preparing for the services. Dr. Nott left a good sum of money and some of his precious pieces for me in his will. I feel so honored but we've been so busy that I've had no time to mourn the loss of this great man.

It is a very dark, cold, rainy, day this January. The memorial service is long, but the burial is brief for the rain is not lettin' up. As people leave his graveside, I cannot move. I say my good-byes to him alone on this hillside at the cemetery. Though it rains, I do not care, for I need to pray one last time for his soul:

"You are free, Dr. Nott, from the pain and the aches in your bones. You are no longer chained to the bent-over achy body of bones. You will be missed by many."

And as I said this I know that if he were here he'd say, "No need, Moses. To be absent from the body is to be present with the Lord, my friend."

I have spent a lot of time with Mrs. Nott and Anna preparing for the grand funeral for this man. I pray for Dr. Nott, my friend, who stands alone as the strongest leader for this college, who influenced our country by sending students into the world prepared to lead our nation, who worked hard speaking and teaching on slavery so that we colored people have a right to own our own flesh and blood, and whose love for his wife was as strong as his love for Union College.

I leave him now on this hillside, at peace with his soul gone off to Heav'n, where he will be lifted by all my ancestors and those who have gone before him.

Chapter Twenty-nine

Going Back to Maryland

It's been a few years since the end of the war and a few months since the President Nott's death. There have been more students coming back to the college. Mrs. Nott is comfortable in the new house, mourning the loss of her husband, but still trying to keep up with her social responsibilities.

Dr. Nott left me and Anna some money and property to build our own home in Schenectady. We now have a lovely home and the pleasure of sitting on our front porch as we watch our neighbors and friends pass by with a wave of a hand or stop by for a sip of Anna's lemonade. With the end of the war, Anna and I have decided that we do not have to worry about slavery and therefore it is time for me to go back to Maryland and have her meet my family.

We will be careful to be safe though, as some people are still set in their ungodly ways. Regardless, I am excited about the visit and sad at the same time. I don't know who's alive and who's dead. I want and need to see my ma and pa but I know in my heart they might be alive they might be dead, but Anna needs to meet them. Anna has been encouraging me that we need to take a train and buggy back to Denton, Maryland.

As we ride the train that runs along the many rivers through forests and mountains and through many states, I am now realizing how much I had to travel by foot to get to freedom. It took many days to escape from the plantation get to Philadelphia and on to New York. Then, missing my connection in Troy, where we never met up with the abolitionists, my error sent me to Schenectady whereupon I met Dr. Nott. My many years of service at Union College, even the name of the college, fills me with warmth.

As we step off the train, tired of the chugging, noisy trip and the uncomfortable wooden seat and the smell of steam, it still was certainly a better trip back south than the trip I took coming north. I had sent word to my family in a letter which train I would be taking and I hope that it had reached them and someone who was kind enough to read it to them.

As we looked into the crowd, I saw the spitting image of my father waving at me and Anna. But as I walked towards him I realized he must have been frozen in time because he looks as young as when I left. We didn't say a word, we just hugged in silence as I felt the salty tears come down my face. He was strong, bigger than when last I saw him, and now I realized he was my brother.

"Well, it's mighty nice having you folks visitin' and I reckon you must be hungry and tired. I have the buggy hooked up over yonder and we will have a bit of a ride to the plantation."

It was my brother and I had to get used to his ways of talking, but that didn't take long.

"We all thought we ain't never see you again, Moses, and we was a glad you made it to freedom. Pa and Ma were so happy when they heard you had made it, or least knew you weren't coming back. Two of our brothers are done passed on, we heard. They had escaped and we be proud because they done fought in the war on the Union side and gave their lives.

They are heroes in our family. When we get to home, there be only three of us brothers left on the plantation. We get good wages from Mr. Murphy. He said we be most trusted of slaves, since we ain't run away. Some of our brothers gone off to Chicago, I hear. All our sisters were sold and I not heard from them since they gone. When Ma died . . . " and he stopped because I had gave such a shout.

"Ma is dead?" I asked, and he shook his head.

"What about Pa?" Brother said, "Moses, it's like this. Ma died before the war ended. She just ain't woke up one morning, but she was happy that three of her children had gone on and got their freedom."

"Pa had one other daughter by another woman after Ma died. He lived to see his daughter reach her first year and he died when his heart gave out. He loved that little girl, her name being Leila. She's now four years old and very small. So you see, it's just us five that I know of—you, me, our two brothers and Leila. Now there's six with Anna. Maybe one day we will all be together again in Heaven. I'm learning a lot 'cause we be going to church."

As Brother was sharing this, Anna was rubbing my shoulders and the buggy was going over the ruts in the road. I kept my head down, with tears just a-coming down as I said goodbye in my heart to Ma and Pa.

We pulled onto the plantation and my heart was racing. I didn't know if I would be welcomed or shot by the Junior Master Murphy. As we pulled near to the house we used to live in, I realized it was barely standing. Brother kept driving past and I saw a small cottage, a little larger than our home on campus, with a vegetable garden in front, a door and some windows.

As we stepped off the buggy and I lifted my Anna off and took time to hold her in my arms for just a minute, someone came from behind and grabbed the back of her legs and we both held each other up. We looked around and there was this tiny girl with big eyes and lots of wild hair. She was hugging Anna and then released her and ran to hug me.

She said, "Hi, brother Moses and sister Anna," as she pulled Anna by her hand and led her into the house. Brother and I walked in and no one else was home.

"Our other two brothers are working the fields until dusk. This is Leila, she is our half sister. We all be take turns minding her, but there are times when she must be left here alone, there would not have been enough room in the buggy for all of us and your belongings."

We looked around and asked where her mother is. Brother took off his hat and said, "Her mother is dead from the pneumonia about six months ago. Now Leila is the only girl around. So she is always excited when she sees a woman since living here with us boys is hard. She is a handful sometimes."

Anna proceeded to sit down and before she even has a lap, Leila is sitting on her and talking about the garden and her doll, which is a rag doll with no eyes and one leg. Brother, laughing at Leila, says, "It's time to head over to Master Murphy and, mind you, we ain't suppose to call him that now, so we just say Murphy sir or Mr. Murphy 'cause he ain't our master anymore. It been right good of him to keep us brothers together.

"He says we are loyal to him, not running off and escaping. And now that the war is over, we built our cottage you see here at the edge of the plantation and he gives us wages. He be a waiting for to see you."

I left Anna with Leila while Brother and I walked over to the master's house. From this distance, I can see that the main house is in need of repair. Some paint and a new roof would be a good start.

As we entered the house it feels so much smaller than I remember. We entered from the back kitchen, which still smelled of good cooking, and headed to the living room. The furniture was in the same places, nothing new, just older and dustier. There in the big chair sat the Young Master Murphy who was as round and as old as the Old Master Murphy and kind of looked like him as well. He stiffened as he stood up and I, not knowing what to do, took off my hat and said hello.

The last time I was here, I had no shoes and an old shirt on. Murphy reached out his hand and I am surprised. I reluctantly put out my hand and he shook it with a strong grip. For a moment he looked five years old and I longed for those childhood feelings. Murphy coughed and said, "Welcome back, Moses. It is good to see you and I see them Northerners been taking good care of you. How be's you since leaving here, with the war and all?"

It's as if I never left, but I'm on a different footing here and now. We ain't equals, but we ain't master and slave. He wanted to hear about my life, so we spent over an hour sharing stories. As we left, Murphy put out his hand and offered to shake one last time. This time I firmly took his hand, looked him in the eye and said:

"It's been a pleasure coming back and I sure hope to be back again," not really knowing if this was true.

As Brother and I left, I saw the old house where we grew up and asked if we can go see it. As we got closer to it, I realized it was just four walls and a tin roof. There was one door and one window with no glass in it. We entered inside and I'm seeing the straw on the floor and Ma at the fire and Pa sittin' in the only chair, wooden with slats, but they are not really there. It is so small, on this dirt floor we all slept with straw and one or two blankets. I wonder were we truly treated better.

We ate with our fingers, only two spoons for Ma and Pa. We had one tin can that we shared to drink from the water pump outside. And we thought this was good living because we were treated better than other slaves. I looked up at Brother and said, "We didn't have a bed no bath, but Ma and Pa made this our home. Yes, indeed, we were treated better than other slaves. But now that I've tasted freedom, I realize we had nothin' but the clothes on our back and even that didn't include shoes."

Brother joins in and says, "We are all much better off without slavery. We are the masters of our lives, no more whippins', no more splittin' up our families. Ma and Pa restin' in peace. We done good work here; we were a family. The war and slavery may have pulled us apart, but we are always together in our hearts. Let's get back to Anna and Leila."

After many days of eating Anna's cookin'—my brothers aren't much of cooks—enjoying her biscuits and apple pie, it was time for us to leave. Leila's hair is plaited with big bows and Anna took time to make her a little shift of a dress long enough to grow into and hide her knocked knees.

As we were about to leave, I could tell the brothers were up to something. They came over to me while Anna was still in the house saying good bye to Leila who was crying so hard about us leaving.

"Moses, we want to ask you something. Leila is our half sister, but we don't take care of her too good and proper, leaving her here many hours of the day and running back to check on her to see if she is fine. You and Anna have no children and you know if you were still a slave, Anna would have been sold away from you for not bearing you no babies.

But we are free now and your Anna is so good to Leila and knows what to do with the girl. Would you be so kind to take her with you and raise her as your own? She won't be much trouble and she is smart and good. What do you think Anna would say?"

As they said this, Anna was coming out the cottage crying as we heard Leila wailin' inside. I looked at Anna and took both her hands in mine and said, "It's right about time we started our family and I think Leila would be a welcome smile in our home."

Anna closed her eyes and caught her balance as I held her.

"The hardest thing I have ever done in my life was to say good-bye to that sweet little thing in there. I'm light-headed, going from heartache to wonder. Yes, yes, let's bring her home and raise her up as our own."

And with that, Anna gave me a sweet kiss and jumped and turning on her toes, she ran back into the house. Suddenly, I heard from the cottage, Leila's muffled cries turned into laughter and giggles, and I knew I now had to prepare for two ladies in my home. I will treat Leila as our daughter-sister and we will raise our family.

As we said our good-byes and headed north with my little family, I knew this would be the last time I'd be back on this plantation. I felt pain and forgiveness as I looked back and saw my two brothers with tears down their face. And as we passed the Murphy home, Junior Mr. Murphy was on the porch waving out to us, and we waved back. As Brother leads the horses, I look in the back of the buggy to cherish my family and there is my wife holding on with dear life to our daughter, my sister, as they talk of the clouds in the early sunlight and the shapes they make.

The laughter brings a warm feeling to my heart as my family is complete. It's a new world, this freedom for our family under one union.

Epilogue

My little daughter/sister Leila is a lovely young lady, who learned a lot from her mother. After Nott's death, Anna and I bought a lovely home on Lafayette Street. As coachman and gardener for the widow Mrs. Urania Nott, I watch over Mrs. Nott to make sure she is safe and help with the goings-on of the house and her company.

After years of suffering from stomach pains in the womanly way, my lovely Anna died on December 12, 1885. During her life here in her hometown, she became very well-respected in the community and the local news paper even wrote in her obituary, "Mrs. Anna Viney was a person of much intelligence and had read a good deal for one of her opportunities. She was sensitive to the wrongs and disadvantages of her colored race and took a practical interest in its improvement. She has done well her humble part through a long life."

This was a very sad time for me, for you see my Anna was a loving, caring woman who waited so long for me to return from Canada. And when I did return, we could not have children. But she did me one better, she helped raise my baby sister who now has grown up with a good education as a free woman.

Leila was my Anna's daughter in all the meaning of a mother and child and they loved each other deeply. Leila did not take the death very well and has paid more attention to my needs since then by cooking, cleaning and all.

Soon after Anna's death, I was faced with the death of Mrs. Nott who I will dearly miss. She was very generous, leaving me in her will Dr. Nott's extension chair, wash stand and table and $1,000 for services as a watchman in her house.

When she was alive, I decided to buy her horse and carriage. She so enjoyed shopping with me driving pass the other women who seemed envious. I went into business for myself. I'm now a coachman for the people of Schenectady and I've driven for generals, bishops, authors and guests who visit Union College.

Since Mrs. Nott's death, I drive the wealthy women in town and one newspaper wrote that "the ladies consider it quite 'chic' to shop with Moses." I gave a little laugh at that, to think that riding with me is 'chic' and at one time I was a barefoot slave living on a plantation where nobody knew about me. Now I'm in the papers.

As for Union College and the boys who attend who affectionately call me "Old Man" I stop by and visit very often. I like to attend the alumni dinner and I dress up in a suit, wearing President Nott's hat and carry the ivory head cane that Dr. Nott left me in his will.

When I go to the programs, it feels good that these young boys who are now men want to shake my hand and greet me. The evening newspaper once wrote that I was the "most noted and picturesque figure on the streets" as we rode from the college to the Armory for our dinner. I do try to walk the campus on occasions, but I've developed the rheumatism and now understand the pain that Dr. Nott's body was going through and the difficulty it is to walk and move my old bones. It seems that I've been in the local papers or the school papers, not sure why I get all the attention. But it was good to read the Daily Union quote when they interviewed me after I retired:

"I have now been obliged to give up on account of my ill health and thank all the citizens in general for their liberal patronage. I used to often hear Dr. Nott tell the college boys that were late to always be punctual and I have always endeavored to carry out this plan in all my dealings with my customers."

One of my most memorable days was the ceremony of the 100th anniversary of Dr. Nott's inauguration as President of the College. The students stood in a long line just to shake my hand. Who would've known I'd be so popular? I was so excited and the crowd was so large, I stood on a chair and showed everyone there Eliphalet Nott's hat and the whiffletree of Dr. Nott's old three-wheeled carriage that I used to drive.

Then I pulled out of the pocket of my jacket the pen that Dr. Nott used to sign diplomas and everyone applauded so loudly I almost fell off the chair. I refused to say a few words 'cause that was not my place and was happy that President Andrew Van Vranken Raymond said, "We must excuse Moses from making a speech; his presence is eloquence enough."

I felt honored for that phrase that I will never forget—my presence is eloquence enough. None of this would have happened without the kind and generous soul of President Eliphalet Nott.

Yes, siree, I miss Dr. Nott, Mrs. Nott and my Anna. We placed a picture of Dr. Nott on our wall of family pictures in my living room. In this room I am never alone for I have pictures of my wife and family and there are times when I hear their voices and conversations we've had in the past.

I am at peace in this room. I take my daily walks around Crescent Park and on the campus. I know I don't have long to live and look forward to joining my Anna soon, but I also must make sure Leila is taken care of. She and I have talked about what she would do when I'm gone.

She is a fine young lady, but she needs to settle down and start a family. She will go back to Maryland and be once again with her cousins and our family there. I will also leave her all my belongings in a will so that she is taken care of, since she has devoted her life to Anna during her illness and now to me.

I have been blessed with generosity and I can honestly say this because of my relationship with President and Mrs. Nott, the love of a good woman Anna, the sweetness of my daughter-sister Leila and the admiration of the boys of Union College. At the age of 91, I know of no other member of my family who has lived this long in the life of freedom and the joy of the Lord— a joy despite hardships that comes from having a sound relationship with Him. As the Good Book says, "Do not sorrow, for the joy of the Lord is your strength."

Newspaper reports on the occasion of the death of Moses Viney.

The Daily Union announced on January 10, 1909 at 11:00 PM the death of Moses Viney: "Death Sets Old Slave Free."

The Evening Star stated "His mental faculties were fine until just two days before his death, and he recognized and conversed with visitors in that time."

Concordienses, the newspaper of Union College announced: "There is no one about whom more memories of by-gone days cling than about this faithful and devoted Negro. It is with sorrow that the Alumni will read of the death of one who has seemed to them to be part of old Union herself."

The Daily Union reporters were in attendance with a large number of people at the funeral and reported the burial of Moses Viney in the Colored Plot of Vale cemetery, where "some colored friends ordered a floral piece for the coffin that spelled out "Free."

Resources for *A Bonded Friendship*

American Public Health Research. 2015 *Nothing to Work without Cleanliness.* www.ncbi.nlm.nih.gov

Andrews, W.L. and Gates, H.L 2000 Slave Narratives. Literary Classics of the United States, NY.

Banjo History 2114 www.banjohistory.com

Boyko, J. 2013 Blood and Daring: How Canada Fought the American Civil War and Forged a Nation. Knopf, Canada.

Buell, B. Feb. 26, 1996 Union College Event to honor escaped slave Moses Vining. The Schenectady Gazette. P. D1-D3.

Carlarco, T. 2004, The Underground Railroad in the Adirondack Region. Macfarland and Co.

2 Corinthians 5:8 King James Version

Daily Union January 10, 1909, *Death Sets Old Slave Free.*

Davis, D.B. 2006. In Human Bondage: The Rise and Fall of Slavery in the New World. Oxford University Press

Davis, D.B. 2014 The Problem of Slavery in the Age of Emancipation. Knopf, NY.

Dibbell, J.B. 2005. Eliphalet Nott on Education and Public Service. Friends of Union College Library, NY.

Garnet Newspaper 1910 – Letter from Nott for Moses Viney. Union College, NY p. 281

Gates, L. 1988. Six Women's Slave Narratives. Schomburg Library of Nineteenth Century Black Women Writers. Oxford University Press.

Harris, A. 2014 Behind the Great Leader: The story and Influence of Urania Nott. Union College Magazine.

Hislop, C. 1995. Eliphalet Nott: An Abridgement of the biography. Union College Press, NY.

History World, 2014. www.historyworld.net
Leviticus 25:45-46. King James Version

Mackel, K. Caroline Office of Tourism, Denton MD

Morrison, M.A. 1997. Slavery and the American West:

The Eclipse of Manifest Destiny and the Coming of the Civil War. U of North Carolina Press.

National Center for Public Policy Research. www.nationalcenter.org

National Underground Railroad Network to Freedom, Easton MD

Negro Spirituals. www.negrospirituals.com No More Auction Block for Me. Go Down Moses. Nobody Knows De Trouble I've Had.

Nott, Eliphalet, Account Book 1855-1859, Special Collections, Union Library

Perseverance Conquers Much: Union College in the final Decade of Eliphalet Nott's Leadership, 1850 – 1859. 2009. Friends of Union College Library.

Philippians 4:6-7. King James Version.

Public Broadcasting Service Organization. www.pbs.org/wgba/aia

Public Broadcasting Service. 2114. Slavery and the Making of America. www.pbs.org/wnet.

Rhythm Bones Central. www.rhythmbones.com
Schenectady County NY History and Genealogy. www.schenectadyhistory.org

Schenectady County Historical Society, NY

Sernett.M. 2002. North Star Country: Upstate New York and the Crusade for African American Freedom. Syracuse University Press.

Somers, W. 2003. Encyclopedia of Union College History. Union College Press, NY.

Stauffer, J. 2008. Giants: Parallel Lives of Frederick Douglass and Abraham Lincoln. Twelver Hachette Book Group, NY

Underground Railroad History Project of the Capital Region, Inc. New York (URHPCR)

Upper Canada Village www.uppercanadavillage.com
Vale Cemetery, Ancestral Plot (formerly Colored People's Plot) Schenectady NY

Van Santvoord, C. and Lewis, T. 1876. Memoirs of Eliphalet Nott, DD.LL.D. For Sixty Years President of Union College. Sheldon, NY

Ward, A. 2008. The Slaves War: The Civil War in the Words of Former Slaves. Houghton Mifflin Co. NY.

Wilson, H.E. 1983. Our Nig: or Sketches from the Life of a Free Black. Vintage Books, NY

Wineapple, B. 2013. Ecstatic Nation: Confidence, Crisis and Compromise, 1848-1877. Harper Collins, NY.

Yetwin, N.B. 2001. The Odyssey of Moses Viney: Part 1: Born into Bondage. Schenectady County Historical Society Newsletter. V37. No. 9-10 (May-June) p.5.

Yetwin, N.B. 2001. The Odyssey of Moses Viney: Part 2 Exodus on the Underground Railroad. Schenectady County Historical Society Newsletter. V37. No. 11-12 (July-August) p.5.

Yetwin, N.B. 2001. The Odyssey of Moses Viney: Part 3: Schenectady's African American Community. Schenectady County Historical Society Newsletter. V38.No. 1-2 (September - October) p.5.

Yetwin, N.B. 2001. The Odyssey of Moses Viney: Part 4: Exile and Redemption. Schenectady County Historical Society Newsletter. V38. No. 3-4 November - December) p.5.

Yetwin, N.B. 2002. The Odyssey of Moses Viney: Part 5: The "Old Man" of Union College. Schenectady County

Historical Society Newsletter. V39. No. 1-2 (January - February) p.5.

Yetwin, N.B. 2002. The Odyssey of Moses Viney: Part 6: Death Sets Old Slave Free. Schenectady County Historical Society Newsletter. V39. No. 3-4 (March - April) p.5.

Yetwin, N. B. 1996. Vale Graves Give insight into Afro-American History. The Sunday Gazette, June 9. P. F3.

Yetwin, N.B. 1998. Profile in Courage: History Teacher Uncovers Story of Ex-Slave's Life in Schenectady. Schenectady Gazette February 21. P. B1-B3.

About the Author

GRETCHEL LINNICE HATHAWAY, PhD, is the Dean of Diversity and Inclusion and Chief Diversity Officer at Union College, Schenectady, NY. As a valued member of the Senior Staff, Dr. Hathaway reports to the President and is responsible for leading the college's strategic plan diversity initiatives with the board of trustees, faculty, administrators and staff. In her book, Dr. Hathaway observes that the story of Eliphalet Nott, president of the college for 63 years and Moses Viney, who escaped slavery and was employed by the College President, was initially brought to our attention by a Schenectady high school teacher and the volunteers at the local Vale Cemetery where both Nott and Viney are buried. Nott took a stand against slavery and set an example for the campus community, by leading both financially and politically with Viney to get his freedom.

What is intriguing about this century-old story of the relationship between Union College President Eliphalet Nott and Moses Viney is that it exemplifies the vision of the present college administration and the message sent to our students. Inspired by the words of Union College's President, Stephen Ainlay, "Drawing from the strengths of our past to guide our future," Dr. Hathaway's focus is to provide educational opportunities and social interactions that will ensure that members of the Union College campus community are culturally competent and engaged citizens of this world.

Dr. Hathaway received her Bachelor's degree in psychology from Manhattanville College (NY), her Master's degree in psychology from Yeshiva University (NY), and her Doctorate in Social Work from the University of Pittsburgh (PA). She has conducted diversity and inclusion, racial and gender bias, and Title IX workshops and programs for professional organizations and at higher education institutions including Swarthmore, Colgate, Manhattanville, Hamilton College, Skidmore, Trinity, University of Pittsburgh, University of Pittsburgh at Johnstown and Union College. Her research interests include diversity, equity and inclusivity in higher education, child and teen physical and sexual abuse, marital rape and spousal abuse.

A social worker by profession, Dr. Hathaway works with faculty, staff, administrators and students to enhance the quality of the academic and social experiences for all who work and learn in educational environments. In addition to her educational and research pursuits, she has published prose and poetry, is an avid lover of gospel and jazz music, has recently taken up painting, and is often spotted driving while singing unapologetically to her favorite tune. Dr. Hathaway lives in Clifton Park, New York, is the proud mother of two children, Stephen Joseph Tyson, Jr. and Rachel Linnice AvelinaTyson.

Made in the USA
Columbia, SC
04 November 2018